TIPS & TECHNIQUES
FOR A NORTHERN GARDEN

SUN, SEED & SOIL

Dan Rubin

BOULDER
BOOKS

Library and Archives Canada Cataloguing in Publication

Title: Sun, seed, & soil : tips & techniques for a northern garden / Dan Rubin.
Other titles: Sun, seed, and soil
Names: Rubin, Dan, 1947- author.
Description: Includes bibliographical references and index.
Identifiers: Canadiana 20230131697 | ISBN 9781989417508 (softcover)
Subjects: LCSH: Gardening—Canada. | LCSH: Gardening—Atlantic Provinces.
| LCSH: Gardening—
 Northeastern States. | LCSH: Gardening—Northwestern States.
Classification: LCC SB453.3.C2 R83 2023 | DDC 635.0971—dc23

Published by Boulder Books
Portugal Cove-St. Philip's, Newfoundland and Labrador
www.boulderbooks.ca

Design and layout: Tanya Montini
Editor: Stephanie Porter
Copy editor: Iona Bulgin

Printed in China

We acknowledge the financial support of the Government of Newfoundland and Labrador
through the Department of Tourism, Culture, Arts and Recreation.

TIPS & TECHNIQUES
FOR A NORTHERN GARDEN

SUN, SEED & SOIL

Dan Rubin

BOULDER
BOOKS

CONTENTS

WHAT WE GROW

FOREWORD
A New-Found Perspective

Gardeners are dreamers. Nowhere is that truer than here in Newfoundland and Labrador. This is not a province of deep rich soils, long warm summers, gentle breezes, fast growth, and guaranteed bountiful harvests. For the northern gardener, this place lies somewhere between torment and a strange paradise. Yet this is where we live.

Gardeners learn from the previous year's successes and mistakes, and then make adjustments to help their plants grow better. If you are new to gardening, you can benefit greatly from sharing in the knowledge of those around you.

Sun, Seed, and Soil is a distillation of lessons learned by Dan Rubin in his own garden, as well as tips gleaned from the many gardeners he knows across Newfoundland and Labrador. He writes about how to take advantage of a garden's particular setting and conditions, how to build soil, and how to grow specific crops.

Family vegetable gardens were a mainstay in rural parts of this province, but they became less common in the latter part of the 1900s,

     DAN RUBIN

until the cod moratorium (declared in 1992) gave thousands of people the free time and interest to revive gardens all around the province. More recently, isolation by COVID-19 has encouraged people to take up vegetable and flower gardening in many more communities.

No matter what happened the previous year, gardeners find hope in the next growing season. In the depths of winter, surrounded by garden catalogues, want overwhelms need as we are seized by the urge to break the boundaries imposed by reason, space, and climate.

Why not try growing magnolias, peaches, grapes, sweet corn, and kiwi in your backyard? Why not, indeed—some gardeners are having great success with them. And if you cannot grow them outdoors, you can always try them inside a greenhouse.

On the island of Newfoundland, winters are not that cold; summers are cool, but summer days are long. Along the coast, we have constant moisture, so gardens rarely need to be watered. Frost-free days can last into October, and the soil never freezes very deeply. Seashores, peaty soils, and well-treed city streets are excellent sources of organic matter. If you don't have soil in your garden, you can make it in raised beds, over time. You can find, or build, a place in your garden to suit the plants you want to grow.

Gardeners in Ontario and the West envy our constant moisture. Gardeners to the south are amazed by our lush cool-weather plants and green lawns. Gardeners in temperate locations are surprised that we have so few weeds and problematic insects. And I won't even mention the raccoons, skunks, opossums, deer, moles, and other pests that gardeners in this province don't have to think about.

In the dark of winter, seed catalogues and plant books can become escapist literature. But they lead us on, to long, enjoyable summer days spent working outdoors. In this strange paradise, gardening provides the perfect workout, and optimism is the best fertilizer.

—*Michael Burzynski*

INTRODUCTION

I make my home now in Pouch Cove, a small town on the rugged east coast of Canada, but this is not where I grew up. During my childhood in Southern California, I learned about gardening alongside my father, Sam Rubin, a visual artist who was a true Renaissance man, knowledgeable about nature, science, art, and society. My father was also an accomplished gardener. In later years, he lived in Hawaii, where he was able to grow tropical fruit.

In the earlier years, on a steep hillside property in Los Angeles, he planted corn, beans, salad greens, and tomatoes. Our fruit trees produced peaches, apricots, and loquats. I have wonderful memories of sitting in the branches of a huge apricot tree, high on the dry grassy hillside, eating sun-ripened apricots. My sister and I picked and ate the lozenge-shaped bright orange loquats even before the exotic fruit was fully ripe.

The photograph of me on my father's shoulders was taken in our backyard corn that mimicked the corn in the larger fields we would find while walking along the hilltop above our house, where residents grew the maize that they had brought from Mexico.

Exposure to the natural world is a gift for any child. In our family garden, I learned to respect living things, from the trapdoor spiders lurking in their woven tunnels to the horned toads that also did their share of insect control. I have carried that deep sense of connection with other living things with me through the years. More than any specific advice, I hope you will share that sense of connection and curiosity as you read this book.

The most important lesson from my early years in the garden is that we are doing a dance with nature. We work with what the world gives us, shaping it to meet our needs, but we should always remember that we are not in control. If we keep that truth in mind, we will constantly find opportunities for better productivity, by studying what is around us and learning how to harmonize with it.

The property that my parents purchased in the early 1950s was a narrow piece of south-facing hillside, with a house originally built for the staff who looked after African game animals kept by the film industry. The steeply sloping land behind our tall, grey, two-storey house had few flat places. Planted years earlier with olive trees and apricots, it was hit by a fierce grass fire that swept up the hill just before we moved in.

Dan on Sam Rubin's shoulders.

Unripe loquats.

DAN RUBIN

Sam Rubin in his garden in Hawaii.

Fifteen years later, when I crossed the valley and climbed the hill across the way as a high school student, even in the middle of summer, I could look back and see the green rectangle that was our backyard, framed by dry, brown hillside. That verdant landscape was the result of learning from nature. It would have been very difficult to bring water all the way up the hill, so my father had carefully planted, from bottom to top, plants that needed less and less water: from corn, tomatoes, and peaches at the bottom, to grasses and succulents at the top, plus the olive and apricot trees—all of which thrived, because our garden was harmonized with the patterns of the natural world.

The author lived in this owner-built, off-grid home beneath the maple trees for 30 years.

In the 1970s and 80s, I homesteaded on an off-grid island in the Salish Sea, north of Vancouver. There I built a home, dug a well, and fenced a large garden. Power was provided by solar panels on the roof. Heat and hot water came from burning wood. Living off-grid on Lasqueti Island helped me learn even more about adapting to the landscape and how to harmonize with the living world.

Then I moved again, to a small coastal outport on the island of

Newfoundland. Here I have presented workshops I call "Creating the Year Round Garden" to hundreds of people at community gardens, the Newfoundland and Labrador Horticultural Society, Salmonier Nature Park, and the staff at our provincial power company. In each session, I learn something new from the participants. The information I share in my workshops can be overwhelming. So I have tried to distill the main ideas and techniques in this book. I hope that, organized in this way, they will be easier to understand and absorb.

In this book I am sharing what I have learned as a gardener, while living in a different climate and location from the place where I was raised. Little by little, I have learned how to meet the challenges of gardening in a cold place, without relying on pesticides and patterns of control that have made much of our agriculture unsustainable. The keys to success with plants, it turns out, are simple and logical.

    DAN RUBIN

If you are an experienced gardener, you already know about the central themes in this book. I hope readers will move through these pages at their own pace to find the information they need. Gardening is a journey, an onward-moving personal adventure, in which successes and mistakes all have lessons to teach us.

My windy waterfront garden in Pouch Cove has been a primary source of learning, as well as food. I am happy to share whatever I have learned, and I am always ready to learn more. If you have questions or new ideas and information, please contact me through my heritage seed company, Perfectly Perennial Herbs and Seeds (www.perfectlyperennial.ca).

Now let's dive into the details, beginning with the three core insights I have gleaned from 20 years of gardening on the wild Atlantic coast of Canada. At the most basic level, it is all about sun, seed, and soil.

SUN,
SEED
& SOIL

1. SUN

Gardeners depend on, and must learn about, the basic needs of plants in order to create the right conditions for growth, flowering, and fruiting. How those needs are met depends on location, type of plant, and the plant's specific needs. Northern gardeners face the challenges of short summers, long winters, and the impact of weather, including cold and strong winds.

Plants are sun engines—complex organic chemical factories that capture light and use it to create food. Through photosynthesis, plants absorb water, carbon dioxide, and soil ingredients to create sugars, proteins, and other compounds essential to their growth. As they do this, they free up oxygen, which they release back into the atmosphere.

For the northern gardener, *sun* means more than just sunlight: sun means *warmth*. By protecting plants from wind and cold, we can expand the growing season, giving plants a head start in the spring and extending production into late fall.

Plants need warmth. In my garden, I build or plant to create protection from wind, even more than from cold. The northern gardener must become a designer of shelter, finding locations and creating structures to provide wind protection.

So how do you do that?

Create a wind shadow. Identify buildings, trees, and bushes that block the prevailing wind and plant in those protected spaces. You do not need solid structures to achieve wind protection. A fence with horizontal slats or vertical fencing, or even a section of netting, will break the force of the wind and prevent windburn, the withering of leaves caused by the constant passage of air currents. My garden has 27 fruit trees and bushes, each planted in the lee of a building or a fence or a large tree.

Build raised beds. Our raised beds, built of untreated spruce and fir 2-by-10s, are 90 centimetres (3 feet) wide and 210 centimetres (7 feet) long. We cut each 10-foot board into a 3-foot and a 7-foot section, which we attach at the corners with strong, rust-resistant 3½-inch deck screws to create a rectangular box. There is no need for a post in the corner when working with boards of this thickness. We place and level each bed, fill it with rich organic soil (more about that later)—and it is ready for planting.

Create protective structures. Raised beds can also provide a stable, strong foundation for additional protective structures. We use materials (often free or recycled) to create cloches, cold frames, and mini-greenhouses to protect plants from wind, retain warmth and moisture, and, at the same time, deter pests. Several basic variations in structure and materials are used to create these microenvironments.

These structures were not lifted from a book of garden designs but are based on simple principles of structural design, using free or inexpensive new and recycled materials. The loads of lumber, plastic, and glass that are dropped off daily at the landfill represent lost opportunities for extending the growing season in any backyard. We regularly find windows, doors, and plastic panels that can be

DAN RUBIN

Peppers grown in a raised bed with wind protection and straw mulch.

used for plant protection are being thrown away by our neighbours. If you search around, you will find the same.

Venting is essential. Once you have enclosed structures, the real issue becomes ventilating on warm, sunny days to release heat and moisture. Just as in a large greenhouse, the temperatures inside smaller structures can become too high, even in cold, windy locations. Visit your garden every morning (a good habit anyway, to monitor plants, to study and learn what they need) and prop open a lid or roll up the cover on a tomato house to regulate temperature based on the current sun and weather conditions.

By controlling heat to provide improved growing conditions, you can create a year-round garden. Another way to create year-round production is with fall planting of cold-tolerant greens in protected beds.

Plant cold-tolerant greens. Lettuce, arugula, spinach, chard, kale, late flowering broccoli and broccolini, and a long list of Chinese

greens, including bok choy, sui choy, feng qing choi, and the mustard relatives mizuna and red mustard, can be seeded in early October. They will sprout and begin to grow in the late fall. By December, when the cold and snow arrive, these plants will be well established. Through the winter, in the icy months of February, March, and April, by simply sweeping the snow aside and raising a lid or opening a sheet of plastic, you will have access to a backyard bounty of fresh greens for a winter salad or soup.

Start seeds early. Start bedding plants in early spring, seeding them in small containers indoors and then placing them under a bank of ordinary fluorescent tube lights, five to six weeks before they are ready to plant out. Even more effective than fluorescent tubes are high-intensity LEDs, although they are more expensive.

We harden off our plants in April and early May, moving them out to the greenhouse or transferring them to the protection of an outdoor cloche, to get them ready for planting out.

Potting on. Normally, once bedding plants germinate and begin to grow, they will have to be potted on (repotted to a larger container) to keep them from becoming rootbound as they wait

DAN RUBIN

to join the rest of the garden. This step can add an extra month of growth to the main garden season. Once the weather is warm and it is time for these seedlings to be planted out, they will be strong and well rooted. If transplanted into raised beds with protective covers, they quickly become established and will be on their way to producing a harvest. The process of potting on lets you start more plants in a limited space, then expand the space they require by moving them into larger plant pots before hardening them off.

Late-season harvesting. Many of the vegetables grown in our gardens will last into late fall and the beginning of winter: flowering broccoli, Brussels sprouts, leeks, Jerusalem artichokes, kale, chard, and some fruits, including apples, quince, and plums. By leaving these in the ground or on the tree to mature, they benefit from collecting as much sunlight as possible.

These strategies for plant protection are grounded in identifying plant needs and harmonizing with those needs. By using the strategies and structures described here, you can extend the growing season by up to two months, produce healthier plants, and increase garden yield while making use of inexpensive or recycled materials.

2. SEED

The second key to northern gardening is careful selection of which varieties to plant. Successful northern gardening depends on selecting plant types that are well adapted to a short growing season and cold climate.

Just 100 years ago, North America had more than 1,000 small seed companies propagating varieties that grew well in a specific region. Many of these local varieties of corn, tomatoes, lettuce, and legumes are now considered heritage plants, because they have been grown in the same place for 50 or more years.

The farmer or gardener who discovered a stray mutation or created a cross with particularly fine qualities would save the seeds and replant them. Over time, all living things adapt and, as they are changed by local conditions, a version of "survival of the fittest" has resulted in the creation of many of the fruits and vegetables that are now widely available. Heirloom plants are these precious locally adapted varieties, also called land races, varieties of proven local value.

Many of the food plants we grow now have crossed the seas more

than once. The general term for this movement of plants, coined by historian Albert Crosbie in 1972, is the "Columbian Exchange." Christopher Columbus and other explorers, including Sir Francis Drake, brought new food plants back from the Americas. This transfer was followed by a return exchange of new plants, animals, and diseases, from Europe to the Americas.

Plants imported to Europe from North America included cacao (chocolate), tobacco, vanilla, peanuts, cassava, squash, quinoa, sweet potatoes, pineapple, the nightshades potato, tomato, and peppers, and the "Three Sisters" (pumpkins, maize, and beans). These crops were then spread across Africa and Asia. The most rapidly accepted animal import was the turkey; Europeans were already hunting wild birds such as pheasants and raising peacocks, chickens, and ducks, imported from Asia. So turkeys were a big hit.

Tomatoes were originally known as "love apples" and it took a long time for them to be accepted because they were considered poisonous. This may have been because the stems and leaves of

DAN RUBIN

nightshades such as potato and tomato are toxic. It took hundreds of years before potatoes became a staple crop in Europe.

New plants were also exported to the Americas for commercial production: sugar cane and coffee, as well as cotton from the Middle East, although cotton was already being grown on both sides of the Atlantic. Other crops followed: apples, peaches, pears, bananas, olives, onions, citrus fruits, grapes, and turnips plus the grains (wheat, rice, barley, and oats) as well as domesticated livestock (cattle, pigs, sheep, and goats). Whether horses were already living in North America before the arrival of the Spanish Conquistadors is a subject of debate.

Over the next four centuries, a wide range of imported grains, vegetables, and fruits flourished in the "New World." At one point, more than 17,000 named varieties of apples were being grown in North America, as Helen Humphreys has documented in her book *The Ghost Orchard*. By the beginning of the 20th century, a rich diversity of plants was found across the continent and, by then, more than 2,000 local seed companies were in operation. By 2022, 75 per cent of that diversity has vanished and only about 250 seed companies remain.

Since World War II, giant chemical companies such as Monsanto and Syngenta have gobbled up the smaller seed houses to dominate the market. After acquiring the seed stock of these small businesses, the larger companies have eliminated thousands of local varieties from distribution and now, of the thousands of types of lettuce, tomatoes, or carrots once grown by gardeners and farmers, over 75 per cent of these cultivars (identified types) have been lost.

Seeking even greater profit through control of the market in seeds, these giant conglomerates have bred hybrids and used genetic modification to create unique genetic types, for which they have claimed patent rights. This will allow these companies to better control and dominate the seed market. This situation is particularly fierce for commercial farmers, where legal action has been taken against those who have allowed patented varieties to appear in their fields, even though the seeds were not purchased by them. Commercial seed cleaning, a traditional business in the Canadian Prairies and the American Midwest, has almost completely vanished under the threat of lawsuits.

As a result, commercial farmers have largely lost the ability to save seeds from their own crops. They are being forced to purchase seeds from Monsanto and the one or two other large companies monopolizing the seed market. This change has had severe negative effects on the web of life, since many of these new commercial seeds have been developed to accept the various poisons used in commercial agriculture.

But there is good news for gardeners. Many of us have awakened to the loss of biodiversity and the need for local adaptation in the varieties we plant and have decided to do something about it.

In the US, Kent Whealey founded Seed Savers Exchange in 1975. In Canada, Seeds of Diversity, a national organization of gardeners, farmers, and concerned citizens, has created regional and national seed banks to keep true breeding varieties going. These precious heirloom seeds can be dried and then deep frozen to preserve their genes, or else they must be grown and harvested annually, their seeds saved and replanted.

As the owner/operator of Perfectly Perennial Herbs and Seeds, a tiny heritage seed company, I am familiar with the work needed to keep this going. Every plant produces seeds in a particular way, so harvesting at the right time and saving seeds has become an area of learning and a passion for me. If you find a valuable true breeding variety worth preserving, you can also join the ranks of seed savers, harvesting and preserving your own seed for replanting, and sharing them with your friends and neighbours.

For the northern gardener, it is crucial to find the right variety to plant. Not all tomatoes are equal. Not all apples are the same. Each plant that is grown, year after year, gradually adapts to local conditions. Aside from any concerns about whether a seed is organic, it is important to add *locally adapted* to the criteria for choosing what to plant.

The easiest way to obtain appropriate seeds is to order them from regional companies that select for local adaptation. In the Atlantic region these include Gaze Seed (Newfoundland and Labrador), Vesey's (Prince Edward Island), Annapolis, Cochrane, Halifax, and Incredible Seeds (Nova Scotia), and High Mowing Seeds (Vermont). Wherever you are located, there will be local seed houses.

You can become an active member of the seed saving community and gain access to thousands of northern adapted varieties by joining Seeds of Diversity. Their website (www.seeds.ca) lists more than 100 large and small Canadian companies from which members can order seeds. The internal catalogue lists thousands of seeds grown by other members. This allows you to order seeds directly from more than 200 fellow growers across the continent. Most Canadian gardeners work with short growing seasons and cold weather; Seeds of Diversity is an excellent source for information about new, cold-adapted varieties.

Each crop comes in multiple varieties for multiple uses. At one time, gardeners selected several types of tomatoes to grow each year: a large tomato for slicing; a pulpy, easy-to-peel variety for canning and sauces; a watery but sweet one for juicing; and a smaller cherry or plum type for salads. The "tomato that conquered North America" was the San Marzano, brought to North America by immigrants from Sicily in the early 1900s, which gave rise to a huge canning industry in California.

Seed packets sourced from large US and Canadian companies that you find for sale in big box stores, supermarkets, and garden centres are generally not the best ones for northern gardens. While they may be cheap and easy to find, the typical tomato varieties (Beefsteak, Sweet Million, and generic plum tomatoes) are a narrow set of standard types that are not necessarily appropriate for our

  DAN RUBIN

more challenging growing conditions. Searching for less common types such as Scotia, Bonnie's Best, and Red Alert can help create bountiful production in the north. The Seeds of Diversity catalogue lists more than 2,000 tomato varieties available from fellow growers.

For a successful garden, seek out varieties that grow well where you live—those with excellent flavour or good storage qualities or that provide a longer harvest. Your garden will become an ongoing experiment as you plant and evaluate different types, record what you have learned (more about garden journaling later), and discover and replant favourites.

Open pollinated vs. hybrid varieties. To effectively select which plants to grow, it is important to know the difference between open pollinated (true breeding) varieties and hybrids. A hybrid is a natural or human-made cross between two distinct varieties. This happens when pollen from one plant is carried to the flower of a different variety by wind, insects, or humans. The new plant's seeds are a mixture of the two original varieties, while the skin and flesh derive from the parent plant. Planting second-generation seeds delivers mixed results. Half of the plants will be the hybrid; the other half will carry the characteristics of either parent A or B. Many hybrids are worth growing and are available from seed companies, but they do not lend themselves to easy home seed saving.

If you find a true breeding type that you like, and you want to save your own seeds, you will need to create an appropriate distance of isolation from other plants of the same species, to ensure that the seeds will remain true to type. But regardless of whether you save seeds or buy them from a good local or regional source, you need to plant the right type for your location and climate.

Plant selection is a delightful pastime, especially in the cold months when seed catalogues arrive. While most seed companies have websites from which you can order, there is nothing quite as

inspiring as settling in on a cold winter's day with a cup of your favourite hot beverage and a stack of seed catalogues. Browsing through descriptions of tomatoes, peas, beans, salad greens, quinoa, ground cherries, celeriac, Florence fennel, buckwheat, or mâche (corn salad) will help you find varieties that are productive and reliable in your location.

Finding the best plants for our climate and soil has become the mission of Perfectly Perennial Herbs and Seeds. Each year, we grow a small selection of plants, focusing on varieties that can help restore food security to local families and communities. So far, we have tracked down an heirloom tomato; a sweet, flat-leafed kale; and local walking onions (giant green onions that grow as a perennial to produce foot-tall onion greens).

DAN RUBIN

Perennial, annual, biennial. It is also important to understand the difference between perennial, annual, and biennial plants. Perennials grow from year to year without having to be replanted. The more of them you plant, the easier your gardening will be. For the rest of your planting, you will choose annuals (plants that must be replanted each year) and biennials (plants such as kale and other cabbage family plants that take two years to go to seed).

Selecting short-season varieties is one way to improve northern garden production. Length of growing season (shown in seed catalogues as *days to harvest,* which usually means from the time they are planted out) is one clue. In addition, the growth characteristics listed in the catalogue will help you decide if a variety will do well in your location, soil, and garden setting (e.g., whether a plant needs full sun, long day length, or rich soil).

The key takeaway: search for those varieties of seeds that are best adapted to your climate and soil. If you replant them, they will continue to adapt to local conditions. The lesson of seed is to look for the right varieties for your garden.

3. SOIL

Next up is the essential foundation for plant growth: the soil. I regularly express my aversion to the term *dirt*, which I regard as a symptom of a basic societal confusion. In common usage, *dirt* means something dirty, something that needs to be cleaned or thrown away. Calling the crumbly brown stuff that lies beneath our feet *dirt* suggests that it is dead and worthless. In my garden, plants do not grow in dirt, or *ground*, a more neutral term used on the east coast of Canada. They grow in *soil*.

This distinction is important. In Newfoundland and Labrador, 1.6 million years ago a wave of glacial advances scraped away plants, animals, and soil, leaving only bedrock in most places. After the glaciers melted, organisms gradually recolonized the land. First came lichens, then Arctic-alpine plants digging their roots into cold rock and gradually breaking it down. As the cycle continued, more plants and animals colonized the landscape, living and dying and breaking it down to form soil. All life returns to the earth, if we let it.

Soil is not inert, dead material. Soil is alive. It is the result of the work of decomposers and the home of the decomposers themselves. Hidden beneath our feet is an enormously complex ecosystem. Billions of organisms live in a square foot of healthy soil and help our gardens to grow. If you recognize, respect, and support these organisms, your garden will thrive and become a place of health and balance, self-sustaining and self-regulating. With the help of the community in the soil, you can avoid turning to the various poisons that have become an accepted part of pest control.

Remember: *You feed the garden, then the garden feeds you.* In other words, keep adding organic matter, enriching the soil with nutrients, and creating a loose soil structure so that oxygen can penetrate and reach everything that lives there. This will support those organisms that make their home in the soil, and they in turn will feed your garden plants. Decomposers break down complex molecules to create smaller, more water-soluble forms that are easier for plant roots to absorb. That is the secret of rich, healthy soil.

Around the world, gardeners, horticulturists, and farmers are rediscovering the value of not digging in the soil. Because we rely on these natural biological communities to provide nutrients for the plants, disturbing them by plowing or digging turns out to be a mistake. The move toward no-till agriculture has begun and is rapidly spreading. As documented in the film *Kiss the Earth*, regeneration of living soil can help us address and even reverse climate change, and this growing appreciation of the full range of organisms that live in soil can lead us toward a more sustainable way of growing our food.

I must admit, I do love the sight of newly turned soil in a raised bed. Digging in the garden is very satisfying. But it is a step backwards, if you want to build long-term soil fertility. This is one reason our so-called civilization has become so dependent on

chemical fertilizers to maintain food production; the natural living agents for rebuilding soil fertility are being too regularly evicted.

The more you know about your garden soil, the easier it will be to create good growing conditions, by tempering the acid-base balance (pH) and amending soil by adding missing nutrients. Consider submitting a soil sample to your local agricultural station, extension office, or government department of agriculture. They will run a series of tests to tell you what nutrients are present, low, or missing; the pH of the soil; and its structural details. With that information in hand, you can begin to improve your soil by adding the needed materials. Your soil will probably lack organic matter, but in some places, rich in accumulated forest soils, inorganic matter, including mud, sand, and grit, may be required.

If, like me, you live on an island known as "the Rock," where soil is thin or absent, how do you garden? You build healthy soil

by adding organic materials from several easy-to-find local sources. This same advice still applies to those living in the rich alluvial soils of the Fraser Valley or rural Ontario, or the thin soils of the Arctic. Building a good garden starts with adding organic material to create soil fertility.

The Old English word for loose, well-balanced soil is *tilth*. Tilth means the right balance of three major soil components: clay, sand, and organic matter. Generally—except for deep, rich prairie soils built up by animals grazing on the grassland over millennia, or soils

     DAN RUBIN

built up by forests and in bogs—soils lack organic matter. Organic matter must be added to create better conditions and support soil organisms and plants.

Soil nutrients. The most important plant nutrients are nitrogen (N), phosphorus (P), and potassium (K), the three numbers found on most bags of chemical fertilizer that refer to the level of concentration of these elements. Nitrogen is essential for the growth of leaves and stems; phosphorus promotes root development, flowering, and fruiting; potassium is critical for water absorption and growth.

Organic matter is generally rich in nitrogen and also supplies a basic amount of phosphorus and potassium. But even more importantly, it contains essential micronutrients needed for plant growth that are not usually found in artificial chemical fertilizers. These micronutrients include zinc (Zn), iron (Fe), manganese (Mn), boron (B), chlorine (Cl), copper (Cu), molybdenum (Mo), cobalt (Co), vanadium (V), sodium (Na), and silicon (Si). Without a trace amount of these elements in the soil, plants will not grow or produce high-quality flowers and fruit. The best source of these micronutrients is natural soil amendments such as compost, peat, manure, maple leaves, seaweed, and marine waste.

Compost. A two-tier compost system—a large backyard bin for garden trimmings and waste, plus an enclosed plastic bin for kitchen waste—allows us to maximize the use of organic materials generated by our home and garden. In our cold, wet northern climate, compost can take up to two years to break down. Chapter 9 explores how to use composting to accelerate the breakdown of plant materials.

Peat. Peat bogs are low-lying forest clearings where water accumulates, leading to the growth of sphagnum moss and other swamp-loving plants. As these plants break down, they gradually fill in the depression, creating a dense mat of fibrous organic matter metres thick: peat. Peat is not rich in nutrients but, when added to the garden, it loosens the soil to create tilth. As peat also tends to be acidic, it is a valuable soil amendment if growing potatoes (which prefer lower pH soil); but when it is added to beds for other crops, particularly brassicas (cabbage family plants, which prefer higher pH), the acidity needs to be balanced by mixing in dolomite garden lime.

When peat bogs are mined and material that has taken millennia to build up is removed, we destroy wetlands that are active carbon sinks and release even more carbon into the atmosphere. Peat use may have to be curtailed in an age of extreme climate change.

Manure. Manure is, of course, animal poop, dropped by chickens, sheep, horses, goats, and cattle. Although bagged, composted manure can be purchased commercially, it can also be sourced from local farmers engaged in animal husbandry and neighbours who keep chickens and goats. Manure is rich in nitrogen (from urine), phosphorus, and potassium. Fresh manure can "burn" plants (causing roots and leaves to dry and wither). Once aged, however, it becomes a rich, dark substance perfect for use in the garden, with only residual odour. Manure can be used as a top dressing around plants or dug into the soil.

Maple leaves. Maple leaves, gathered each fall, are an excellent source of plant nutrients. Every year, city streets are lined with bags filled with leaves for curbside pickup. Homeowners, many of them gardeners, do not realize that they are throwing away a major source of soil fertility. At the Memorial University Botanical Garden here in St. John's, maple leaves are considered "black gold": they turn into the rich, dark soil essential for garden beds. Maple leaves are not a primary source of nitrogen, but they do include the other necessary elements. To release these nutrients, it is best to shred and compost the leaves after gathering them.

Maple leaves are a rich source of plant nutrients because maple

trees are nutrient factories. Their deep roots reach out wider than their branches to search for the best minerals, dissolve and pump them up the trunk, out along the branches, and into the leaves, where photosynthesis occurs. From these minerals, plus oxygen and water, the tree makes everything it needs. When leaves change colour in the fall and drift down, they carry the results of that activity. We rake up the leaves, run a mower over them, and add them to our compost to take advantage of all the work that the trees have done. We also use maple leaves as mulch in the fall: layering them on our overwintering crops of garlic, onions, and leeks. The leaves provide a layer of winter insulation, then break down to feed the soil. Maple leaves should be at the top of a gardener's list of free local soil amendments.

Leaves from other deciduous trees are similarly useful, but oak leaves and needles from evergreens contain too much tannin and acidity to be an effective garden addition.

Seaweed. The rugged coastline of the island of Newfoundland offers easy access to seaweed, another valuable, free resource. All

forms of seaweed can be gathered when they wash up on the beach. Seaweed is a significant source for plant micronutrients, because organisms living in the sea gather and concentrate the minerals in sea water. Kelp and the rockweeds that grow in shallow waters are ideal sources of essential plant nutrients.

Many local coastline gardeners harvest seaweed, gathering it from piles deposited high on beaches in spring—where it has been washed free of most of the salt by rain and snow—stuffing it into bins and bags and bringing it home. Seaweed can be dug into the soil or set out in the sun to dry, then crumbled and added to garden beds. Once the seaweed has broken down, soil organisms further decompose the nutrient molecules to make them available

     DAN RUBIN

to plant roots. In outport communities, adding seaweed to potato drills and vegetable gardens was a traditional practice. Seaweed can significantly reduce soil pH, and the resulting acidity can be balanced with the annual addition of dolomite lime.

Marine waste. Long-time residents of Newfoundland and Labrador (livyers) traditionally used fish waste as a major source of micronutrients. What was not split, salted, and dried on platforms (flakes) was carried home. In Pouch Cove, it was normal for each home to dig a compost pit into which plant materials and fish waste were thrown. In some areas, fish waste was layered on vegetable beds, or dug in, in the fall. Once composted material had broken down, it was carried to the fields where families grew root vegetables and other crops.

For those who live near the sea, gathering seaweed and recycling fish waste is straightforward, but what about gardeners who live inland? Fortunately, some individuals and small businesses are turning marine materials into bottled concentrates that can be shipped anywhere. Our favourites, made locally, are Natural Gardener Seaweed Booster, made from water-composted kelp by Brian Yager, a garlic farmer in Ferryland, and NL Marine Organic fish emulsion, produced by a local company headed by Diane Hollett.

The incorporation of peat, manure, seaweed, and fish waste into soil to create a healthy living ecology is an example of connecting with the way the natural world moves everything in cycles. Gardeners should recognize this cycling of nutrients as an engine, moving molecules and water and oxygen, powered by the sun's energy, feeding everything that grows in the garden.

One caution: avoid, as much as possible, those plastic sacks of mystery soil sold by big box stores. Recent stories from fellow growers have confirmed that no one really knows what is in them. Reports of disappointing harvests and dead plants have been surfacing where some materials labeled "black earth" or "marine compost" have been used. Not all brands are unreliable but the truth is, there is little or no regulation of the bag's contents. Whenever possible, avoid bagged soils and use local, organic sources for building garden fertility. We start our seeds in commercial sterilized potting soils, available by the bale from trusted sources. Potting soil is a soil mix that uses sterilized peat. We avoid the rest.

Mycorrhizae. Underground fungal threads known as *mycorrhizae* (my-ko-RY-zay) connect and feed your garden plants. In a mature forest, every tree is connected and communicates with every other tree, sending messages through these fine threads provided by more than a thousand types of fungi. Forest ecologist Suzanne Simard has conducted years of research on this topic, which she shares in her book *Finding the Mother Tree: Discovering the Wisdom of the Forest*. The benefits of these fungal threads are immense. In the forest, mature "mother trees" act as nursemaids and active protectors of young growth and the underground network connects every plant. Simard reports from her own garden:

> The mycorrhizal network played a part in this dance, my garden's network shuttling nitrogen from the nitrogen-fixing beans to the corn and squash. And the tall, sunny corn transmitting carbon to beans and squash it was shading. And the squash sending the water it had saved to the thirsty corn and beans. My garden thrived.

In healthy, living soil, several hundred species of fungi make their home, connecting with plant roots and exchanging nutrients.

The power of mycorrhizae was revealed to me during a visit to the Campbellton Berry Farm, where proprietor Philip Thornley dug his fingers into wood chips lining his paths to reveal a dense

DAN RUBIN

network of white fungal threads directly linked to the roots of his black currant bushes. These connections form an intense pattern of nutrient pathways joining fungi to his berry plants. The wood chips, he explained, create a perfect habitat for these mycorrhizae that double plant growth and berry production.

Layering wood chips as mulch on your garden paths is therefore a great idea. Although they take up nitrogen as they break down, they give it back three times over, in the long run. Wood chips create the perfect home for these amazing fungi that will restore soil fertility as they directly feed garden plants.

Use natural materials to build and nurture living organic soil. In this book, we explore how to work with the basics of sun, seed, and soil. But before launching into the details of how to grow each type of garden plant, let's take a closer look at the cycle of activities that make up the garden year.

THE GARDEN YEAR

4. WINTER

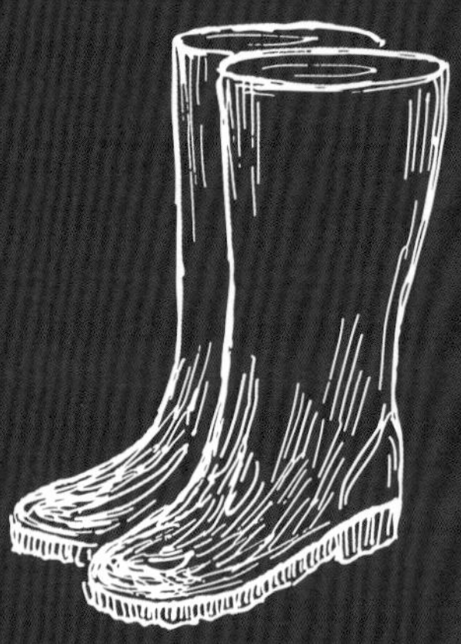

Think of winter as garden dreaming time. Once the fall production season is done and winter weather arrives, you can relax, appreciate your well-stored harvest, and plan for another yearly cycle. Here are some winter activities to keep you busy during the cold months and help you move into another productive garden year.

Reflection. Winter is the time to read, study, and plan. Every year brings unique challenges, successes, and failures—and winter gives you time to examine these. If you keep a garden journal (which we recommend), you can review the past growing season to extract insight. If a plant or a bed did not do well, ask "Why?" By repeatedly asking that question, and not assuming that you know the answer, you will think more deeply about possible factors—weather, soil quality, pests, the need for better protection, or new plant varieties.

Garden clean-up. Winter is also a time to clean up the garden, burn pruned branches (to create bio-char to feed the soil), and note areas or structures that need renovation or repair.

Bring perennials indoors. Perennials growing in plant pots and containers can be sheltered indoors, inside your home or in a greenhouse. Dormancy is a normal part of the year for many plants, particularly perennials.

Mulching for winter protection. During winter, cover garden beds with a layer of mulch—wood chips, compost, manure, or maple leaves. If your garden is as windy as our waterfront property, weigh the leaves down with screens, tarps, or boards to keep them from blowing away. Layer organic materials on top of beds. Seaweed is one choice; it breaks down during the winter. Manure can also be applied at this time of year. It is best to avoid mulching with hay, as it may contain grass seeds, does not provide much thermal insulation, and can create hiding places, in the spring, for slugs and snails. In a cold, wet environment, hay becomes a favoured medium for mould as it breaks down.

Seed ordering. A vital part of garden dreamtime is the luxury of browsing through seed catalogues. Even though it may be more efficient (and cheaper) to order from a single source, studying seed catalogues from three or four (or half a dozen!) suppliers will reveal critical differences among varieties of seeds and plants.

In the past several years, we have noticed an increasing rush to purchase seeds and plant materials. Stock for late fall/winter planting (for example, fall-planted garlic and flower bulbs) sell out early, although some companies may have inventory available into late winter. As long as the freeze has not arrived, and the ground can still be worked, bulbs can be planted deep for frost protection and covered with a blanket of mulch for insulation.

Ordering seeds presents so many tantalizing possibilities. Studying seed catalogues is also a chance to learn more about what grows best in your location and climate. The search for short-season, cold-adapted plant varieties is a never-ending journey. Even though we may not order every iris or lily offered in a catalogue, scanning its pages is almost as satisfying as walking into the greenhouse at our

DAN RUBIN

favourite plant nursery when the flowering annuals are in full bloom.

Garden plan. Developing a garden plan is highly recommended. It helps you think critically about how you will move your plants from bed to bed, year after year. Our garden plan is a rough sketch of our beds and planting areas, renewed each year, as we figure out where the new plantings will go. Although some gardeners question the need for rotating plants if the beds are supplemented annually with organic nutrients, moving crops in a cyclical pattern reduces the persistence of spores and disease organisms and allows soil to recharge its levels of nitrogen and other depleted nutrients.

Houseplants. Well-heated homes offer the possibility of growing tropical and semi-tropical plants in containers, including citrus, olives, and avocados. Meyer lemons (a cross between citron and pomelo, created in China) will grow indoors and produce fruit if they are planted in good-quality, well-drained soil. Other citrus species, including tangerines, calamondins, and kumquats, can also be grown indoors. Figs bear fruit if grown indoors or in a greenhouse; olives and avocados generally do not. Decorative plants also thrive indoors if they receive the right amount of water and light.

5. SPRING

Spring is the time of rebirth. For gardeners, it is a time of preparation. The following activities can help you prepare for the intensity of summer and reduce hard work during the rest of the year.

Repairs. Before the growing season starts, you can identify and replace or repair structures that are broken or worn out, and you can organize and order new materials.

Clean-up. Garden clean-up involves removing debris to prepare soil for planting. Remove faded old growth. Old plant material and debris shelter slugs and other pests: remove it from beds and into the compost. But try to protect the yellow silk puffs that conceal spider eggs (your friends in controlling garden insects) and the overwintering brown chrysalis that shelters butterfly larvae that emerge as pollinators later. Mulch can be left on beds to protect the top of the soil and will continue to break down.

Turn your compost. Compost works better and breaks down more quickly if it is well aerated. To fold air into the mix, turn the compost with a digging fork or make holes through the pile. A well-

aerated compost pile also smells better.

Make a garden plan. Many gardeners diagram what they plan to grow in each area or bed. Even better, follow the lead of Welsh organic gardener Huw Richards and create a month-by-month plan to encourage succession planting. Most gardeners rotate crops from year to year to avoid exhaustion of key soil nutrients and plant diseases that hide in the soil. Referring to our garden plans for the past 10 years gives me a clear idea of what we have grown and how we have moved our plantings.

Add soil amendments. Add organic matter (compost, manure, grass clippings, maple leaves, and seaweed) to garden beds and dig it in or, even better, top-dress with it. Spring is one of the best times to add materials that break down through the growing year, releasing nutrients little by little.

Mulching. As we have begun to adopt a more sustainable, no-dig method of gardening, we rely on mulching, adding organic

     DAN RUBIN

materials to the top of the soil. As well as enriching the soil, mulching beds with grass clippings, leaves, or compost creates a protective layer that prevents the germination of unwanted wild plants. Mulch retains moisture and gradually breaks down to feed the soil. After our neighbours' first mowing, we accept their lawn clippings, perfect for mulching around young plants in spring.

Seed selection. As winter loosens its hold, continue to browse seed catalogues, check your garden plan, and make final decisions about which varieties you will grow. Look for plants that provide prolonged harvests. Order seed as early as possible. Seed orders take a few days or weeks to arrive—you simply cannot order too early.

Seed starting. This is the most essential spring work. Starting seeds indoors under lights allows you to extend the growing season by at least a month. We plant the first round of seeds in March, beginning with brassicas, squash and other cucurbits, as well as some hardy herbs. We start the rest of our seeds indoors in April and early May. In warmer parts of Canada and the US, seeds can be started even earlier.

In general, start seeds in pots no smaller than 10 centimetres (4 inches) in diameter, or into cell packs, placing one seed per cell and up to four (one in each corner) in a 10-centimetre-diameter (4-inch-diameter) pot, using only sterilized soil (to avoid damping off, the fungal disease that causes new plants to wilt and die) or your own homemade soil mix (combining peat, sterilized compost, and perlite or sand). You can also use recycled food containers of various types and sizes if you punch drainage holes in the bottom.

A soil blocker is a device that compacts potting mix to create a block of soil ready for planting. Soil blockers can free you from purchasing and washing plant pots. They allow you to compress soil mix to create a shape that will hold together, without using a container or plant pot. Soil blockers come in different sizes, so you

can create small soil blocks for your seed starting, then move the block into a larger soil block, for potting on.

We do not use peat pods, egg cartons, eggshells, or other small containers for our seed starting because almost as soon as the seeds sprout, these tiny containers become too small and can stunt root growth.

Timing is critical: start seeds approximately three to four weeks before they will be planted in the garden or greenhouse. If you plant more than one seed in a container, pot them on into larger containers, after they sprout but before they are garden-ready.

Succession planting. The practice of planting more of the same plant, or different varieties of the same vegetable, at successively later dates in the same bed is called succession planting. It produces waves of harvestable food through the growing season. By planting the same type of seeds more than once, successive harvests will mature throughout the summer. If one round of planting is lost (because of damping off, frost, or other factors), then the next generation will fill the gap. This is an effective way to boost garden production and also provides a form of crop insurance.

Weeding. Weeding may be the least favourite garden activity,

DAN RUBIN

but it becomes more manageable and enjoyable if you are working with raised beds that are not too wide and are easy to sit on. We can go into the garden on a pleasant morning, sit and sip coffee or tea (held in one hand), while weeding an entire raised bed with the other hand, in 15 minutes.

What to do with the weeds once you pull or dig them out? Add them directly to your garden compost. Even better, turn them into weed tea by placing them in a 20-litre (5-gallon) bucket filled with water. Over three or four weeks, the weeds will rot, creating a potent (and very stinky) weed tea full of concentrated levels of all the nutrients that the weeds have collected with their persistent roots. Dilute the concentrated weed tea 1:10 with fresh water to avoid burning garden plants. Water beds with that or use it as a foliar spray, misting it onto the leaves of vegetables, to boost growth.

At a fundamental level, we need to change our attitude toward the wild plants known as weeds. They belong in the garden—but not necessarily in the vegetable bed—and they become a valuable fertilizer during the growing season.

Tree pruning. Pruning tree branches is best undertaken

while the trees are dormant. Once the leaves emerge, any pruning is termed summer pruning, which has a different impact on tree growth and form, discouraging the re-growth of branches. While trees are dormant, before their leaves emerge, take a close look at them, particularly at your fruit trees, and prune to help them achieve a healthy shape and to provide an easier harvest.

First, remove unwanted limbs (broken, diseased, crossed), then do a second round of cuts to open the centre of the tree to allow light and air to more easily penetrate and promote health. When removing a large branch or limb, first cut it at least 15 centimetres (6 inches) from the branching point. Make a second cut to leave a smooth, clean cut with no stub. This two-step process avoids damage and allows the tree to easily heal, avoiding penetration by disease or pests.

Prior to their use, sterilize pruning tools with a strong bleach solution to avoid spreading fire blight (a bacterial infection that can cause trees to wither and die) and any other bacterial or fungal diseases. To prune major branches or remove trees, call an arborist.

Dormant oil. Spring is also the time to apply dormant oil to fruit

DAN RUBIN

trees to prevent scale and mites. Spray oil on branches and leaves while trees are dormant, just before the buds open. This work can be done by an arborist, but as the spray is not toxic, you may wish to do this yourself. The oil kills pests by coating and suffocating them, so it is safe to use around other living things. Generally, dormant oil is mixed with water before it is sprayed. Various dormant oils are available at local garden centres.

Garden journal. If you have not already started a garden journal, this is the time of year to begin one. It is a great way to learn from your garden. Record your daily garden observations and activities. Starting in spring, record growth and plant production, visits by birds and pollinators, daily weather events, and the succession of flowers.

Maple tapping. Spring is the time to tap maple trees. Basic equipment includes a drill with a bit (usually 10 millimetre [3/8 inch]), spiles to insert into the hole in the trunk, and buckets, bottles, or a system of tubing to gather the sap that runs when the temperature moves from below to above freezing as the weather warms up. The hard work is making the syrup, which requires hours to boil down the sap.

On the island of Newfoundland, only red maple and mountain maple are native; most of the maples growing here are the European species: sycamore maple (*Acer pseudoplatanus*) and Norway maple (*Acer platanoides*). Even though the true sugar maple found in New England and Quebec is rarely seen in our area, all maple trees provide natural sugar.

Sap will run when the ambient temperature rises above freezing, because it is the alternation of temperatures below and above the freezing point that tell the trees that spring is on its way. After the sap stops running, the spiles can be pulled and the tree left to heal the hole you have made. The sap, once it is thick and boiled down, is easy to store if you have saved recycled bottles for storage.

6. SUMMER

Thanks to the tilt of the earth's axis relative to its path around the sun, the north experiences longer days and shorter nights in the summer and the opposite during the winter. Our short summer— shorter and more intense the farther north one goes—is the prime time for food production. With longer days and increased warmth and sunlight delivering optimum growing conditions, plants grow quickly, mature, and go through flowering and fruiting cycles.

Summer is a time to focus on creating the best growing conditions. Optimizing warmth, moisture, and soil nutrition is critical. Gardeners respond to weather challenges, including heavy downpour or no rain, temperature variations, strong winds, as well as competition from wild plants, pests, and diseases. These critical activities can help meet many garden challenges:

Weeding. Keeping garden beds and field rows free of unwanted wild plants generally requires cycles of removing or smothering plants. But wild plants actually deserve our deeper understanding.

Except for a few truly invasive species, wild plants build healthy

soil by sending their roots down deep into the ground to search out key nutrients and micronutrients and bring them to the surface as part of their own growth. When these plants die back each winter, those nutrients are deposited on top of the soil, where they feed other plants. The role of wild plants as soil restorers is part of the natural cycle of plant succession, a process of cyclical renewal that started when the glaciers retreated. Wild plants and decomposers are responsible for the thin skin of soil in which food is grown. Soil building continues today.

Think of the word *weed* as a verb, not a noun. A weed is not a type of plant, but a label based mainly on ignorance and habit. Think of them instead as wonderful wild plants. Even as you remove them from cultivated areas, remember that they have value. When you find dandelion, chickweed, pigweed, and other species in your beds or vegetable rows, you can also make a conscious decision to leave them there. Many of them are edible wild greens. Weeding can be redefined as a series of choices, allowing you to fine-tune

    DAN RUBIN

your beds as you decide which plants to remove and which to leave to grow and add to the food supply.

Among the wild plants that we leave to grow for later harvest is lamb's quarters (also known as goosefoot or pigweed), an excellent steaming green, closely related to spinach and quinoa. If left to grow tall, along with cultivated crops, especialy under the protection of floating row cover (white woven garden fabric known as remay), or in a cloche or hoop house, lamb's quarters develops a tall stalk supporting thick, succulent grey-green leaves that are ready for harvest when the plant is a foot tall.

Chickweed, with its thin, wiry stems, lobed leaves, and white flowers, is a delicious salad green. Harvest it along with early dandelion leaves (before they turn bitter) to add variety and flavour to salads. Wild sorrel's small lance-shaped leaves are also edible and add a sour tang to salads.

While many are still engaged in the endless struggle of trying to achieve the perfect lawn, they may have forgotten that dandelions are a source of food: early greens were traditionally eaten as spring salads in Newfoundland; flower buds can be pickled like capers if harvested before the flowers open; and dandelion root, dried, roasted, and ground into powder, is chicory, a coffee substitute.

In late summer, we harvest and dry pineappleweed (*Matricaria discoidea*), wild chamomile that grows along roadsides and in the gravel of our driveway. Its distinctive yellow flower nubs are easily identified by their smell. We mix their dried flowers and feathery leaves with mint and lemon balm to create a soothing Triple Tonic Tea mix.

Learning about wild plants is an exciting journey, and with field study and a bit of coaching from an experienced forager, you will discover a range of berries, wild greens, and herbs that can be added to your food supply as they pop up in your garden.

Even though we appreciate these plants, we do remove them from our beds so that garden plants do not have to compete with them. Weeding can seem like a lot of work, but your life will be easier if you follow some simple advice.

First, don't do it all at once. Pace yourself: weed one area at a time and choose pleasant cool mornings to focus on identifying and removing unwanted plants. Our raised beds are no more than 1 metre (3 feet) wide, built from 2-by-10 wood (which is actually about 4 centimetres [1.5 inches] thick). The thick edge provides a comfortable place to sit while weeding and eliminates straining your back as you reach across the bed.

Second, removing weeds calls for a special technique, to be polished and perfected with practice. Slide your fingers down along each side of the stem of the unwanted plant, dig your fingers into

DAN RUBIN

the soil, pinch the main stem below the surface for a better hold, and then twist and pull to remove the plant along with its roots. Weeding when plants are immature is always easier than when their roots have taken a deep hold in the soil. If you have waited too long and the plant is well rooted, digging with a garden fork or trowel will loosen the roots.

The satisfaction of a well-weeded bed is the payoff, aesthetically pleasing as well as practical, since it frees your crop to grow stronger. To make pulling up plants and their roots easier on your hands, wear gloves and keep a hand trowel or digging fork handy for the hard-to-remove ones.

The plants you have removed can be a prime source of natural fertilizer: simply drop them into a 20-litre (5-gallon) bucket filled with water, where they turn into concentrated plant food! Immersed in the water, they rot and release a wide spectrum of nutrients that their persistent roots have searched out in the depths of the soil. As already mentioned, the result will be weed tea. Dilute it (1 part weed tea to 10 parts fresh water), then water your plants with it or spray it onto leaves as a foliar spray. A warning: weed tea is very smelly, so it's a good idea to place the bucket well away from your back door.

You can also add these pulled plants to garden compost, where they will rot along with the brown kitchen material to create rich organic material. Layering and patience, the right mix of green (nitrogen-rich) and brown (carbon-rich) materials, and moderate moisture are the keys to good composting.

Watering. Choose the right time of day to water your plants. Early morning and evening are more effective than during the heat of the day, to avoid temperature shock and to minimize evaporation.

     DAN RUBIN

The key to effective watering is to water deeply. Soak plants to ensure that the water has penetrated deep into the soil. Just because the top layer looks wet does not mean that the job is done. Deep watering stimulates plant roots to follow the water downward and creates a root web that is efficient at extracting nutrients from deeper soil layers to produce stronger growth.

We give each of our raised beds a full minute of flow. After spraying water over the surface, we poke a finger down to the second knuckle to make sure that water has penetrated deeply. Sometimes a second watering of the same bed is needed, but it can take a few minutes for water to soak in and reach the deeper soil.

If you can set up a catchment for rainwater, it is better to use rainwater to water your garden than tap water. Alternatively, you can fill a barrel or bucket from the tap (municipal treated water) and let it stand for several hours to allow the chlorine gas to escape. Soil nutrients such as compost or weed tea can be mixed into the same barrel or water tank to fertilize plants as you irrigate.

Depending on how hot it has been and how many days have passed since a rainfall, watering the garden may be a daily routine or may be done less frequently. In general, soaking beds and rows thoroughly with a sprinkler or hand-held nozzle means that you may be able to skip a day or two between waterings. One sign that you need to water: plant leaves droop in the heat of the day.

Better than spraying or sprinkling water through the air, where a portion is always lost to evaporation, you can install a drip irrigation system. If you have the time, inclination, and resources, this will save water and decrease the work of watering. Drip irrigation requires planning and careful design and works best if beds or rows are level. The advantage: small amounts of water are consistently delivered to the soil at the plant's base or alongside rows, where it soaks down through the soil to reach the roots. Drip irrigation supplies, including perforated hose, control valves, filters, and timers to turn water on and off, are widely available. Regular monitoring for blockages is required; these can occur if sediment or other materials collect inside the hose and block holes in soaker hoses.

In our large, intensively planted garden, I don't mind spending an hour watering, since it is a pleasant relief from other work and gives me time to observe and study the plants.

Watering in the evening rather than morning encourages mould and other plant diseases if water stays on leaves during the night. If you water late in the day, allow time for the leaves to dry out before night falls. Tomatoes particularly do not like water left on their leaves. It is generally better to soak the soil around tomato plants rather than spraying water on the whole plant.

Protection from wind and cold. Protecting plants from wind and cold is essential in a place where it can snow in June and drop below freezing even in July. Wind can be an even greater threat to plants than cold—but we have found ways to protect them.

We have turned our open garden beds into raised beds. Wooden frames filled with rich organic soil provide a convenient, sturdy foundation for various shelter structures. Many were built with inexpensive, free, or recycled materials such as wooden boxes with lids (cloches) and hoops covered with plastic or floating row cover. More complex structures include a tomato house—a mini-

DAN RUBIN

greenhouse built from dimensional lumber, with a peaked roof. The plastic-covered tomato house can be opened on sunny days and when the weather is warm and closed overnight or when the weather is cold or stormy.

Windburn from exposure to strong winds can damage plants. Protecting plants from wind helps them grow tall and strong. Creating microenvironments protects plants from strong winds, even during the summer.

Mulching. Adding mulch around established plants also helps them thrive. First, mulch discourages weed growth by blocking the sunlight that tells wild plant seeds it is time to sprout. Second,

DAN RUBIN

it retains moisture, decreasing the need for watering. Third, it moderates soil temperature on both hot and cold days. And finally, as it breaks down, materials in the mulch feed the soil. We use a range of natural materials for mulch: grass clippings, shredded garden waste, and wood chips. Wood chips pull nitrogen from the soil as they break down, but they give it back three-fold; if your soil has been tested and is rich in nitrogen, wood chips are an excellent mulch.

Summer harvesting. Summertime harvests begin with the earliest greens, and continue with the first peas and beans, followed by tomatoes, summer squash, and then root vegetables. As you harvest these crops, particularly new carrots, small turnips, leeks, and broccoli, you can thin plantings to release more grow space for what remains in the bed. It is best to harvest in the cool of the day, or immediately before use, to ensure freshness. The core benefit of having a garden is the ability to harvest when food is at its peak of ripeness and maximum nutritional value.

Pest control. During the growing season, some plants may not grow as well as expected, due to insects, slugs, and disease, among other challenges. Part of the summer garden routine is keeping these problems under control. Tackle pest issues without turning to biological poisons by using natural methods. First, healthy plants are always more resistant to pests and disease. Second, use simple methods to control pests when they do appear. In most cases, removing affected plants or leaves from the garden, discouraging insects from laying eggs by covering crops with floating row cover, and watering with sea water once a week can determine how seriously your plants are affected by pests. The best form of slug control we have found is the evening slug hunt, when we find and remove them from garden beds.

7. FALL

As fall approaches, we continue harvesting produce to be transformed into food. Remove crops as they mature. For example, cabbage is usually harvested whole and stored over winter. Leeks, radish, and carrots are pulled whole, thinning to allow the remaining roots to grow larger and thicker. But leafy greens can be harvested more gradually and continually.

The earliest pickings, other than the wild plants that appear in spring and summer, are greens for salads, soups, and stews. Most of what we gather from these plants are their leaves—lettuce, bok choy, spinach, kale, chard, and other brassicas—harvested by breaking off the outer leaves for salad. These plants continue to push tender leaves out from the centre throughout the late summer and fall, offering successive harvests of crisp, green food. Other leafy crops such as onion greens can be similarly harvested, leaving the plant in the ground for a late, final harvest after the earlier harvests of outer leaves.

Some plants are grown for their edible stems, including rhubarb, asparagus, kohlrabi, celery, celeriac, and lovage. Others are harvested

as mature flowers or flower buds: broccoli, broccolini, cauliflower, artichokes, and others. Fall harvests can include potatoes, corn, peas, beans, squash, and cabbage and the root crops sweet potatoes, turnips, and carrots.

Root cellar: Some root vegetables can be left in the ground and protected with mulch, to be harvested in the coldest months and into the spring. Root vegetables, onions, garlic, squash, and other crops can be cured and stored in a cool, dry place for months. Most root vegetables store well in a root cellar, but this does not include squash, onions, or garlic, as these become mouldy if not stored in warmer, dryer surroundings.

Root cellars are a traditional form of food storage and protection

     DAN RUBIN

Root cellars in Elliston (left and centre) and Pouch Cove (right), Newfoundland and Labrador.

on the east coast of Canada that takes advantage of the fact that soil retains warmth and can provide thermal insulation from winter weather. Root cellars are holes dug in the ground, often protected by a building over them, with a ladder leading down into the storage space. They may also be dug into the side of a hill. The hole is enclosed in walls of timber, stone, or concrete to create a cool, dry storage space for the annual harvest. Root cellars need to be vented to allow gases to escape, but otherwise are sealed to keep them dry while providing protection against extreme cold, thanks to the insulation of the surrounding soil.

Root cellars are a simple form of refrigeration that was a normal part of household food storage for centuries. Any strong container

buried in the ground can provide earth-insulated storage for a harvest. A basement cold room can become an in-house root cellar if it is well insulated and the temperature kept above freezing.

Fall planting. During the rapidly shortening days of fall, succession planting of cold-tolerant garden plants to overwinter and provide a year-round supply of healthy food is possible. Two keys to doing this: plant early enough that the greens are well established before the deep cold comes, and create winter protection (cloche, covered box, or other enclosure) to keep out the wind and the worst of the winter cold. If you do this, you can harvest greens that survive in colder conditions through December, January, and February.

Even if they wilt with a hard frost, many greens become crisp again once it warms up even a little. Winter temperatures become more challenging the farther north you go and the longer the cold lasts. The solution: design double-covered, well-sealed structures with extra layers of protection. But even in an unheated greenhouse, it is possible for fall planting to establish crops that will overwinter and provide food through to spring.

Fall is the time to plant hard-necked garlic, onions, and flower bulbs, placing them deep in the soil for winter protection. Plant garlic and bulbs at least 8 centimetres (3 inches) deep. We mulch our garlic beds with thick layers of maple leaves weighed down with

DAN RUBIN

a tarp stapled to the edges of our raised beds, to provide an extra layer of winter protection. In the spring, the cloves begin growing again and we remove the tarp, but leave the maple leaves to rot down and feed the soil.

Fall clean-up. Once harvests have been gathered, cured, and stored, the final act of the garden year begins: clearing away plant debris left by the growing season. Leave plant materials until spring or clear them away down to the soil. Compost what you clear away, to create new plant food. Freezing temperatures may keep this material from working down until it warms up again, but plant materials can sit on the compost or be shredded and layered as mulch on your beds where they insulate the soil.

Harvesting fruit. No garden cornucopia is complete without fruit. We have had success with strawberries, raspberries, apples, pears, plums, cherries, peaches, grapes, kiwis, haskaps, gooseberries, currants, and elderberries. Once well established, these bushes and trees go through their annual cycles of fruit production. Although they do not necessarily produce every year, by adding more than 24 fruit plants to our garden we have generated a harvest of berries, pomes (apples, pears, quinces), drupes (peaches, apricots, nectarines, almonds), plus rhubarb and other vegetable crops that mimic fruit in their acidity, flavour, and uses. Some of this fruit is stored for eating fresh; others are used to make jams, jellies, and preserves. Each year we produce several hundred bottles of fruit wines, which we ferment, bottle, and store in our basement. Fruit can also be dried using a dehydrator for long-term storage.

The key to producing a reliable fruit harvest is to plant the right varieties in the right place. We can harvest big, juicy, golden peaches because we planted the right variety (Reliance Peach, grafted to root stock from the Himalayas) in a location sheltered from the wind. Each of our trees and bushes has been selected for cold tolerance. This has meant bountiful harvests of cherries, plums, and apples from our well-established, northern-adapted fruit trees.

Maple leaves. Fallen maple leaves are a prime source of soil nutrients. Trees gather the best plant foods from the depths of the soil. We have found we cannot locate our garden compost near them because it becomes matted with maple roots sucking all the nutrients from the compost. We rake up the leaves, run a mower over the piles, and compost the resulting shredded leaf mould. Most deciduous tree leaves can be similarly used, but oak leaves have too much tannin. Maple leaves provide some nitrogen but are mainly a source of carbon and a wide range of micronutrients.

Making bio-char. Bio-char is charcoal that is added to the soil to increase fertility: the tiny spaces inside partly burned wood create shelter for the bacteria, fungi, and insects that are primary decomposers. To make bio-char, we burn dried branches and twigs in a 170-litre (45-gallon) metal drum, with holes for air intake in the bottom and sides. We put the fire out with water as soon as the material has burned down. We save the resulting lumps of charcoal and dig them into beds or add them to compost. This helps us avoid putting extra carbon into the atmosphere, instead sequestering the carbon in the soil and turning it into plant food.

Chipping branches. Layering wood chips thickly (up to 22 centimetres [9 inches] deep) on garden paths achieves several benefits. First, it keeps weed seeds from germinating, because the wood chips block light. Second, it creates a perfect habitat for fungal mycorrhizae that spread through the warm, wet chips. These

DAN RUBIN

fungal threads are not only good at breaking down wood chips but they plug directly into plant roots, creating a symbiotic partnership, exchanging nutrients in both directions, to benefit fungus and crops. This symbiosis occurs in a forest or any healthy plant community: all parts of the living world work together to create balance and health. Healthy plants, fed by the additional nutrients supplied by fungal mycorrhizae, are more resistant to pests and diseases.

If you have access to a chipper, turn the branches saved from pruning during spring and summer into wood chips. If you do not own a chipper and cannot rent one, contact a local arborist or a company that clears under power lines. These contractors may be looking for places to deliver the chips.

Overwintering. Some plants can be left in the garden and harvested through the winter. Kale, chard, broccoli, and other brassicas tolerate some frost, if sheltered from wind, snow, and ice. Protect overwintering plants by adding a thick layer of mulch, or enclose them in cloches or cover them with row cover, placing the white fabric over individual crops or entire beds. This will allow you to harvest edible greens, even in the coldest months.

TIPS
AND
TECH-
NIQUES

8. BUILDING HEALTHY SOIL

The Old English word *tilth*, like many traditional words, has lost its original essence and now means the general quality of cultivated land. But its essence is a deeper, historical appreciation for soil that has a proper balance of sand, clay, and organic matter. Each of these materials is essential. Sand provides minerals and creates a looser structure; clay contributes finely broken-down minerals that are more soluble than sand; and the organic matter, derived from the decomposition of living things, contains essential nutrients in soluble form. With a balance of all three, the soil feels and smells rich and alive. Creating tilth is one way to think about building healthy soil.

Get your soil tested. A soil analysis determines which components are present or absent, along with the soil's acidity or alkalinity (pH) and a basic report on its structure. Healthy garden soil has a neutral pH, good aeration, and a rich mixture of organic matter. Soil analysis, done by universities and agricultural extension offices, is generally not expensive. In Newfoundland and Labrador, the provincial agriculture department offers this service at minimal cost. Send a sample for analysis—you will gain a much better understanding of your garden's basic growing medium.

Add organic matter. Most garden soils lack looseness and benefit from adding organic matter. Adding organics is not difficult or expensive. Purchase a load of triple mix (compost, peat, and topsoil) or well-rotted manure from a reputable local source. Ordering "topsoil" is not a good idea, as this term has no fixed meaning and the delivered product can be anything from good garden soil to a rough mixture of sand, roots, rock, and little else.

To create healthy soil, you will likely need to add organic matter. A good start is a load of peat, although peat bog mining has become an environmental concern in recent years. Although peat adds few organic nutrients, it does create looser soil. An even better source for soil fertility is manure, particularly sheep manure, which we prefer over horse or cow manure, as it has fewer weed seeds and richer nutrients. Chicken manure is potent, and high in nitrogen, so it must be well aged to avoid burning plant roots; it adds little in the way of carbon or fibre.

But other sources of nutrients can build soil quality. One of the best is maple leaves, or those of any deciduous tree (except oak leaves, which are too high in tannin). Thanks to the wide spreading roots of maple trees, their leaves contain a rich harvest of major and minor nutrients.

Marine sources. Seaweed and marine waste are rich in essential micronutrients. In addition to the three primary chemical elements for plant growth, rooting, and flower and fruit production (nitrogen, phosphorus, and potassium), plants also need smaller amounts of the metallic trace elements: magnesium, iron, copper, boron, selenium, iodine, and manganese. For good production, potatoes, for example, must have magnesium; beets need boron.

     DAN RUBIN

When you top-dress with seaweed or composted marine waste, you add a time-release fertilizer that will feed your garden, as these materials break down.

Many gardeners in Newfoundland and Labrador rely on seaweed for productivity, some drying it before adding it to their gardens, others digging it in or top-dressing with it, each fall. The other option: make seaweed tea, using the same method as for the weed tea, by immersing seaweed in a bucket of fresh water for up to two weeks.

But the most valuable of any form of organic matter to build soil fertility is compost made from your garden waste and household organics.

Moisture. To support growth, soil needs adequate moisture. Densely packed clay soils resist water percolation; they need to be broken up by the addition of sand and organic materials. It is important for soils to drain well, but at the same time, garden soil needs to retain some moisture to support root growth. If the soil is too wet, roots drown or rot and die back. Healthy soil has a balance of moisture retention and drainage. The key: add organic matter—it

Seaweed and caplin are valuable soil amendments on the east coast of Canada.

acts as a sponge, holding water better than sand or clay, in balance with the other ingredients, to create tilth.

If standing surface water appears in an area, drain it. Ditching, culverts, and weeping tile are options to create water flow: start at a low point to collect water and create a channel to carry it to where it is needed.

Northern gardens are more likely to receive too much water than too little. By thinking creatively and critically about where water collects in your garden, you may decide to create a sump or a pond to store water or collect it in barrels or tanks to save it for irrigation. As seasonal drought becomes more common due to changing weather patterns, water storage will become more essential.

Aeration. Important to healthy soil, but often ignored, is the access of oxygen to feed plant roots as well as the many creatures that comprise the soil community. Without open spaces in the soil, roots cannot penetrate and seek out nutrients, and worms, insects, larvae, bacteria, and fungal threads will not thrive.

Improving the access of oxygen into soil is challenging if you are moving toward no-dig production—if you stop cultivating the soil, it can become compacted. One way to counteract this is to use a broad fork, a digging tool with a row of long thin tines, or an ordinary garden fork. Simply slide the tines down into the soil and pry. This action punctures the soil to a depth of 30 centimetres (1 foot) or more, creating deep, narrow slots to allow oxygen to penetrate.

Add charcoal. Another way to encourage oxygen penetration is to mix in bio-char, in recognition of the role it plays in restoring soil fertility and sequestering carbon.

Charcoal supports soil fertility because it adds carbon directly to the soil; the lumps break up the other soil materials, creating gaps; and, most importantly, the burned wood has an abundance of microscopic pores that become homes for bacteria, fungi, and tiny insects that burrow into the soft charcoal. By creating a suitable habitat for these soil organisms, charcoal is a major contributor to the living communities that restore fertility, providing better retention of soluble nutrients absorbed into pores of the charcoal. It also shifts soil pH toward the basic side.

Mycorrhizae. We have already explained the importance of encouraging fungal threads to inhabit your garden soil. Three main ways to do this: avoid using poisons, especially fungicides; apply a thick layer of wood chips to pathways and around beds; and maintain a minimal level of moisture to support their growth. The interplay between fungi and plants is an important foundational process for soil health.

Soil is a living community. A living community of organisms make their home in the soil beneath your feet. As these organisms move through the soil, they break it up and aerate it. As they break down and decompose materials, they make soil nutrients more soluble and thereby more accessible to the plants' roots. These organisms guard against invasive pests, consuming them and keeping pH and nutrient levels in balance to resist their incursions.

SOILSAVER
CLASSIC COMPOSTER
MARK IV

9. COMPOSTING

The foundation for all growth in the garden is the soil beneath your feet. If you recognize that soil is alive and that it shelters a complex community of organisms working to break down the materials you add to it, your work as a gardener will become much easier. Your partners are the fungi, bacteria, worms, insects, and arachnids that make their home in living soil. They will repay you in soil fertility.

One of the best ways to build soil fertility is by creating a compost pile to recycle household and garden wastes. I am not a good composter. My compost pile takes longer to break down than it should. I have learned much about composting from a master composter: as creator of The Homestead at Flatrock (*facebook.com/flatrockhomestead*), David Goodyear has identified the key steps to making hot, quick-working compost in a cold northern climate.

The essentials are simple: good compost starts with a balance of green nitrogen-rich materials and carbon-rich brown stuff; it should have a moderate level of moisture and be sheltered from rain, ice, and snow to keep it from becoming too wet and cooling

down. In the series of roofed bins that Goodyear builds, it easy to turn the compost to aerate it, and, as he moves it from bin to bin, it breaks down, leaving behind partly composted materials for further decomposition. His triple-bin compost system helps him complete the rapid breakdown of composted material to create fine, rich soil.

While Goodyear's compost is breaking down, its temperatures can approach or even pass that of boiling water. One indicator of good composting is the heat generated by aerobic bacteria as they break down plant materials. Compost fires can begin when grass clippings are piled up and left to dry, but a compost pile will not burst into flames if it is well moistened. Installing a temperature sensor in the middle of the compost pile allows you to track the internal temperature or you can tunnel into the middle of the pile from time to time to check the internal temperature with an oven thermometer.

What happens inside a compost pile? Oxygen-loving bacteria consume and break down the complex compounds and break up the structures in the organic material. As they do this, heat is released

    DAN RUBIN

and the material becomes a loose organic mix. Once the compost cools, worms, insects, and other creatures move through it, breaking it down further and aerating it. Worms speed up this secondary breakdown, particularly the red wigglers recognized as masters of composting. If worms do not appear in your compost, find a local source or order some online. Their presence indicates healthy soil. When you harvest compost, screen out the worms and return them to the empty bin.

Roofs over Goodyear's triple-bin system make it possible for him to control the level of moisture by adding water with a hose or watering can as needed—and preventing rain or snow from making the compost too moist. By using these simple techniques and by paying attention to what his compost needs, Goodyear has compost that is ready to be used in less than a month. In my sloppy backyard bins, without a roof, full breakdown can take more than a year. But the compost is still fabulous once it is ready.

We isolate garden waste from kitchen scraps. We compost the kitchen waste in a black plastic cylinder supplied by our provincial Multiple Materials Stewardship Board. You can find a local municipal, provincial, or other source that provides this device. The tall, tapered black plastic cylinders have a tight-fitting lid and a port at the bottom for removing finished compost.

Into this container go the accumulating contents of the compost bucket that lives inside a cabinet beneath the kitchen sink. To keep our kitchen compost from attracting rodents, we do not put meat, fish, or dairy into the container. But all other food

Household kitchen wastes go into these plastic composters.

scraps, bits of paper, eggshells, and fruit and vegetable peels go in the compost, where they slowly break down. Food scraps and peelings break down faster if they are mixed with such nitrogen-rich materials as grass clippings; we add these too when they are available, layering them between deposits of kitchen waste. We also add layers of maple leaves.

Some gardeners worry that composting will attract rats or mice or that their compost will stink. But well-aerated compost with no meat, fish, or dairy does not create a rotten smell, and if the composter is sealed on the bottom (ours sits on a concrete pad, not on bare ground), it is not as accessible to rodents. If you are worried about unpleasant smells, place the composter farther from the house. Composting is key to a healthy garden.

Because our larger compost pile for garden wastes, weeds, and trimmings is filled solely with plant materials, it is problem-free. These garden materials—prunings, plants removed from the garden (preferably free of weed seeds), small branches, grass clippings, and dried maple leaves—are layered in a much larger rectangular compost bin built from recycled shipping pallets.

One caution about shipping pallets: they may be free and easy to work with, but some have been treated with a fungicide that kills beneficial fungi and contaminates compost. To ascertain if a pallet has been treated, look for a code stamped on the wood: HT means heat-treated. If you see this label in Canada, the pallet has not been treated with methyl bromide, used to kill pine beetles. If it is labeled MB, do *not* use that pallet for your composter. Methyl bromide, a neurotoxin, should be avoided for your own safety and that of the soil.

A composter for garden wastes is easy to build with untreated pallets.

We have built a double-bin compost system for garden waste. Once the first bin is full, we leave it for a year or more for the materials to fully break down while we fill the second bin. By the time the second bin is full, the original bin is generally ready to be emptied and the finished compost moved to garden beds to feed the soil. Any leaves, twigs, branches, or other intact materials can be transferred to the second bin to continue decomposing. We use three shipping pallets to create the back and sides of each bin, with a fourth pallet or wire mesh panel for a front gate. Using pallets makes it easy to assemble a 1-metre (3-foot) cube enclosed by wooden slats on all sides to hold garden waste. If the front panel is hinged or attached with loops of wire, the front gate can be swung open when it is time to turn the compost or harvest material for use.

Using compost in the garden. Applying compost is the easy part. In the spring or the fall, finished compost can be screened and added to garden beds to feed the soil and increase plant health and food production. Organic gardeners regularly dig compost into beds as part of the ongoing work of feeding the soil. Even if the compost contains not-yet-broken-down materials such as small twigs, eggshells, or food remains, these ingredients loosen and aerate soil as they continue to break down.

A few years ago, we created a 1-metre-tall (3-foot-tall) filled with compost that has produced magnificent crops: in the first year, potatoes, then onions, then squash, and now, in its fourth year, some of the largest garlic bulbs we have ever grown.

Our society's system of industrial agriculture strips soil nutrients and ships them away as harvested crops. When a farmer in Ontario, California, or Mexico harvests and exports corn, beans, tomatoes, or other crops, they also export their soil fertility. Whether the crop is grown with chemical fertilizers and pesticides or with soil amendments labeled organic, when it arrives at your local retail store after travelling thousands of miles, the net effect is the same: these vegetables are made up of soil nutrients harvested from the farmer's field and shipped elsewhere.

The peel of a store-bought banana, carrot, or potato contatins a portion of those soil nutrients. That is one reason why composting kitchen wastes is so valuable. Rather than being part of a food system that is actually a food sewer turning good food into irretrievable landfill, you can harvest the nutrients in these scraps and peelings and return them to the soil in your own garden.

Restoring soil fertility is the primary goal of regenerative agriculture, a movement rapidly spreading across North America and around the world. By raising grazing animals that deposit their manure, planting cover crops, and integrating wild plants into the production cycle, living soil can be rebuilt where depleted soils now exist. Regenerative farming and gardening feed the soil, restoring fertility and health. Planting in rich organic soil is the key to building a garden that resists pests, drought, and other challenges.

Vermicomposting. One more composting option to consider, particularly if you live in a small house or apartment and do not have any yard space, is vermicomposting. With a plastic bin for a container and worms as the active agent, household kitchen wastes can be composted rapidly indoors, where it is always warm. You will need a cabinet or corner where you can locate a large bin. Purchase a plastic storage bin with a tight lid. Drill rows of breathing holes into two sides for aeration. Start with 1 litre (4 cups) of soil and a handful of shredded newspaper. Add red wigglers. Deposit kitchen wastes into the bin, alternating food scraps with handfuls of shredded paper. The worms eliminate noxious smells as they move through the bin, turning kitchen scraps and cellulose into compost.

Once the bin is full, let it stand for a week or two to allow the compost to finish breaking down, then harvest the compost by

screening it, removing the worms (which have multiplied in the bin) and returning them to the empty bin with a starter mix of soil and shredded paper, to restart the cycle. Search for "worm composting" online for advice from people who are vermicomposters.

The lasagna method. For a no-dig approach to gardening, consider the lasagna method. Compost as a top dressing for beds and garden rows provides soil protection, retains warmth and moisture, and blocks sunlight to keep weeds from sprouting, while it continues to decompose to feed the soil.

Top-dressing garden beds with alternating layers of compost and other plant materials layered on top of the soil creates a system in which nutrients trickle down to reach the plants' roots when they are irrigated or when it rains. Adding compost layers on top of layers of maple leaves and seaweed feeds the plants, letting natural decomposition create time-release fertilizer. Layering materials on the top of the soil saves effort and reveals the value of letting nature do the hard work.

10. RAISED BEDS

Our most valuable lesson upon moving to the cold, windy east coast from the banana belt of British Columbia's Gulf Islands was the value of growing in raised beds. While some crops (potatoes, carrots, and other root vegetables) may grow better with in-ground cultivation, raised beds offer significant advantages for gardeners in a northern climate. Planting in raised beds makes it possible to extend the growing season, build soil fertility, and ease garden work.

Building rich soil. Because soil quality is the basis for healthy plants, good growth, and good production, the gardener's main task is to build a rich, organic soil mix. A raised bed defines the space in which to do this. The box makes it easier to screen soil (the rocks and gravel can go into the paths); add compost, manure, and seaweed when you prepare beds for the winter, so that they will be ready to plant in the spring, then cover the surface with mulch.

Protection from wind and cold. The garden box also can serve as a wind barrier to protect your garden plants, blocking or deflecting the wind. A second box of the same dimensions as that

holding the soil can be placed on top for additional protection.

Foundation for protective structures. With the raised bed in place, it becomes easy to erect hoops to support coverings holding in warmth and moisture or to build a mini-greenhouse fastened to the raised bed. Raised beds are an essential way to create micro-environments that allow northern gardeners to defy the challenges of a cold climate.

Easier to work in. The edge of a raised bed box built from (nominal) 2-inch lumber offers an easy place to perch while working in the garden. Making the work easy means you are more likely to do it; raised beds contribute to pleasure and create efficiency in the garden.

Raised bed design and materials. Our standard raised bed

    DAN RUBIN

is built out of dimensional lumber. We purchase two 10-foot lengths of 2- by 10-inch untreated lumber for each frame, then cut each piece into a 90 centimetre (3 foot) length and a 210 centimetre (7 foot) length. Because we use thick wood, we do not need corner posts; we attach the boards to each other to create rectangular frames, fastened with 3½-inch deck screws for a durable joint.

Why do we use untreated wood? Even though manufacturers and retailers assure us that the new generation of treated wood is safe to use, they still recommend that wood treated with a fungicide be handled with gloves when building, and we would rather not use anything that kills living things close to where we grow food.

In the past, other materials and chemicals deemed safe (think

DDT, thalidomide, Roundup) have negatively affected the health of humans and other living things. Following the precautionary principle, we prefer to be safe, not sorry. This means that our wooden raised bed boxes have a life cycle of six to seven years before they succumb to rot and must be replaced. We prefer knowing that fungi are alive and at work in the soil, since they bring so many benefits to the growth in our garden.

The wood known as juniper in Newfoundland, also called larch, is a strong, rot-resistant wood that is ideal for long-lasting raised beds. But it is brittle and may split if holes are not drilled before inserting screws to join planks.

While some people build beds that are 120 centimetres (4 feet) wide—and even though that size is recommended in the gardening method known as square-foot gardening—we find this is too wide for easy garden work. If you have to bend or step into the bed to reach a plant, you are working too hard. After 20 years of experimenting, we have figured out that the maximum width for ease of access from both sides of a raised bed is about 1 metre (40 inches). We generally make our garden beds 92 centimetres (3 feet) wide.

    DAN RUBIN

However, any size of raised bed is better than none. It allows you to organize your garden into targeted growing areas so that the beds can become part of a system of annual crop rotation to avoid depleting the soil of key nutrients while eliminating persistent plant diseases that may lurk in the soil year after year.

Raised beds provide a clearer idea of the space required to meet your needs for a particular crop. One of our raised beds produces more lettuce than one family can consume. After giving lettuce away to our friends and neighbours, we have learned to mix and match when we plant salad greens. In a single bed, we may mix lettuce, spinach, kale, arugula, chard, and mustard greens. That one bed becomes a continuous source for a scrumptious salad mix that varies with each harvest.

Adding a second box with a hinged lid, on top of the raised bed, enables us to plant cold-tolerant salad greens in late fall. Once they are established, we harvest them all winter. At the end of December, we can sweep away the snow and pick a fresh green salad. Through the ice and snow of February or in the hungry month of March (as Newfoundlanders and Labradorians say), we have fresh vegetables waiting to be picked.

When we moved to the east coast in 2002, we saw few raised beds; now they are everywhere. We acknowledge the leadership of Nova Scotia garden guru Niki Jabbour, whose books and videos on year-round gardening have inspired many of us. Word has spread by other means too. Thousands of gardeners have built raised beds, making their gardens more productive and extending the growing season.

A variety of materials can be used to create raised growing spaces. Some of our raised beds are framed by dry stone rock walls. Other gardeners have built raised beds with bales of straw or enclosed them with galvanized metal. One local gardener's backyard contains more than a dozen bathtubs that have been turned into container gardens filled with soil and vegetable plants. Raised beds can be made from recycled wooden window frames, sawmill slabs, and recycled building materials.

This is where one's ingenuity and desire to be a producer rather than a consumer can be given free rein. For a polished and elegant raised garden, use dressed lumber and paint the outside of your beds. For a less expensive, funky but functional approach, repurpose discarded materials to create a first-rate grow space.

     DAN RUBIN

Raised beds can be built with
a variety of materials, many
of which are free or recycled.

11. SHELTER STRUCTURES

Simple shelter structures can be added to protect plants in raised beds from wind and cold. You do not need to be an engineer, carpenter, or trained craftsperson to build these. A few simple tools and common sense turn inexpensive or free materials into adaptable enclosures that stand up to wind, rain, and snow. Possible variations, in a range of sizes, include cold frames, cloches, row covers, and mini-greenhouses.

Cold frame. A cold frame is a wooden box covered with a glass window or transparent plastic lid that traps the sun's warmth and keeps out the cold. Used to harden off plants to prepare them to grow in the garden, or as a long-range strategy for year-round growing, cold frames range from a small box or frame with a recycled window on top, to full-sized raised beds with a recycled shower door or plastic panel for a lid. Both versions are easy to design and build, convenient to work in, and easy to move.

So much is thrown away these days from building renovation, including single-pane windows replaced by double-glazed units,

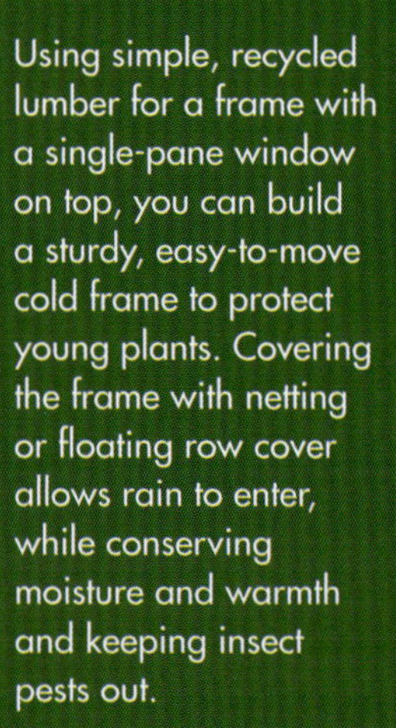

that stacks of windows end up in the dump. By contacting companies that do this work, or by staying in touch with neighbours who may be replacing their windows, it is not difficult to accumulate a collection of windows to be turned into cold frames or to find enough to build a complete greenhouse. As your collection of recycled glass builds up, the hardest part may be explaining why "all those windows" are stacked up behind the house. Once they become part of your food production plans, that question will be answered positively.

Here is a simple recipe for a moveable cold frame: Find a recycled, single-pane window, then measure and cut four 25-centimetre (10-inch) boards to match the window dimensions. Assemble the boards into a box using 3-inch deck screws. Attach the window to the top of the box with standard cabinet hinges along one edge. The hinged side should be placed toward the prevailing wind; strong gusts can catch the edge, flip the window open, and break the glass. If you live

     DAN RUBIN

in an exposed, windy location, add a latch to securely fasten the open edge of the window to the box.

The cold frame rests on the soil in a sunny, sheltered spot. It protects the plants inside it, helping them survive and adapt to colder temperatures, as they harden off in preparation for planting out. One caution: on even a moderately sunny day, the air inside the cold frame can get very hot. Once it is higher than 30°C, plants may wilt or even die. Monitor the temperature inside the box and carefully prop the lid open on sunny days to prevent overheating.

Some gardeners design cold frames that are taller on the north side, thinking that this will gather more sunlight. However, the only factor that determines sunlight access in high-latitude locations is the seasonal sun angle at a given time of year, which determines the length of the shadow cast by the south-facing side. But building one side of the cold frame higher does allow taller plants to fit inside the box.

Cloche. The word *cloche,* derived from the French word for "bell," originally meant a glass dome placed over plants, in the traditional agriculture of France during the 18th and 19th centuries, protecting them from cold. Market gardeners in the areas around Paris also used a system of hedges or walls to block wind and these glass domes extended the growing season in their relatively cool climate.

A cloche is any small moveable transparent covering to enclose and protect plants, or a glass or plastic dome placed over an individual plant. This creates a microenvironment warmer than the surrounding garden space. Using cloches and row cover to extend the growing season allows earlier planting and later harvest. Adding a cloche is simple with raised beds. We assemble a second garden box, the same size as the bed below, built with untreated 2 by 10 lumber, and place it on top of the box that holds the soil. You do not need posts in the corners to fasten down the box because its weight will make it stable

Raised bed frames can be stacked, placing a second box the same size on top. A hinged lid makes it easy to moderate the interior temperature.

in all but the fiercest wind. This top shelter box can be moved from year to year, along with your crop rotation.

For even better protection from weather, the top box can be equipped with a lid, built from 2- by 3-inch lumber, and covered with 6 mil plastic stretched and stapled to the wooden frame. Just as with a cold frame, on a sunny day you will need to open the lid to prevent overheating. During the growing year, we go from opening the lid during the day when the sun is bright and closing it at night or when it is grey and cold, to leaving it propped open all day and night during the warmest months. As fall approaches, we go back to the open-during-the-day, closed-at-night routine to regulate the warmth inside.

DAN RUBIN

Covered beds. Covering garden rows and raised beds with floating row cover also creates shelter. Lightweight garden fabric or plastic sheeting will retain warmth and extend the growing season. Various forms of support can make it possible to open it during hot or sunny days. A simple ridgepole, raised on posts at the end of the row, or supported at intervals down the centre, can have fabric draped over it, held down at the edges with lumber or strapping. Be sure the hold-downs will withstand gusty wind conditions. If it is not sturdy enough, the options described below can provide additional shelter for effective protection from wind and cold.

Avoid using landscape fabric. I have an aversion to "landscape fabric," that black or dark brown woven material that many gardeners incorporate into their beds, placing it beneath a layer of soil in the belief that it will block weeds. We have frequently had to dig landscape fabric from under all sorts of plants in our work as garden designers, and we have noticed that it does not effectively block weed growth, as promised by those who manufacture and market it, because roots penetrate and become entangled in it; the fabric can damage plants in raised beds if placed beneath the bed when the pores in the woven fabric become clogged with dirt particles and block effective drainage.

When that happens, garden plants can drown in the wet soil; and because it is woven plastic, you have no idea what may leach into the soil when it breaks down. Once it is buried and roots have grown through it, removing this fabric becomes a nightmare. For all these reasons, it is best never to use landscape fabric except at the surface of the soil. If you plant through holes in the fabric, it serves as a form of mulch and is easy to remove after use.

Floating row cover. The white woven garden fabric called remay (brand name Reemay) is deployed above plants as they grow, rather than below the soil. It offers significant benefits in northern

Floating row cover can be draped over plants to protect them from cold and insects.

gardens, when used as floating row cover. First, it retains moisture, creating a moist space that many plants, especially brassicas and cucurbits (cucumbers, squash, melons), love. Rain can penetrate the fabric to reach the soil. Second, it retains heat: sunlight passing through it creates a gentle warmth, but it also breathes out excess heat to create optimum growing conditions. Third, it keeps out insect pests, particularly such flying insects as the cabbage white butterfly that will lay eggs that turn into the so-called cabbage worm (actually a caterpillar). For all these reasons, covering beds or garden rows with floating row cover draped over plants, hoops, or frames is a favourite plant protection strategy.

Grades of floating row cover range from lightweight sheets (not recommended because they tear easily in the wind and cannot reliably be reused a second year) to the heavier woven fabric used in commercial agriculture that can be purchased in large folded panels, or by the foot, cut from a wide roll. The heavier version is more effective in a windy location and lasts longer. Check with local suppliers or contact a Co-op store to purchase the proper grade. The goal: create a tent over growing plants to retain heat and moisture without openings or gaps that let in flying insects.

One approach to installing floating row cover involves building a sturdy wooden frame over a raised bed by adding vertical supports tied or nailed to horizontal strapping, with the fabric draped over it. The fabric can be rolled out over the frame and held down (on the downwind edge) by fastening it to a length of lumber heavy enough to tension the fabric, but light enough to easily roll up when you

     DAN RUBIN

need access to the bed. We find 2-by 3-inch (5- by 7.5-centimetre) lumber the right weight for this use. Staple the edge of the floating row cover to the wood, then add a second layer of strapping, screwed down through the edge of the fabric, to secure the fabric.

Another strategy is to drape floating row cover over hoops of metal or black plastic pipe. We cut lengths of 2.5-centimetre (1-inch) black plastic water pipe 2 metres (6 feet) long, whittle both ends of a 30-centimetre-long (1-foot-long) dowel or piece of 2.5-centimetre-square (1-inch-square) square wood into a round peg, then insert a wooden peg into both ends of the pipe. Each end of the pipe can then be pushed down into the soil to anchor it. Hoops are installed at 60-centimetre (2-foot) intervals down the entire length of the bed to provide support for the fabric. They can be stabilized with wire pegged down at one end of the bed and then wrapped twice around the midpoint of each hoop and fastened down at the far end, to form a strong ridge line, holding up the fabric. With that arrangement in place, floating row cover or clear plastic can be stretched over the frame and held down along the long sides of the bed with lumber, metal pegs, or rocks.

Depending on wind conditions, you may need to find a way to keep the lightweight fabric or roll of plastic from being peeled off in strong winds.

If you use plastic sheeting, pay close attention to the amount of heat being retained, even on a cold day under clear skies. Just like with cloches and cold frames, too much heat can "cook" plants and discourage growth. Open the ends of the rows to vent heat and moisture on a clear, sunny day, even when the outdoor air temperature is low.

Mini-greenhouses are wood or metal frames covered with plastic sheeting or glass panels—miniature versions of a full-sized walk-in greenhouse. Although they may be too small to stand inside, they offer a substantial year-round grow space that is warmer and more secure from windburn than the rest of the garden. We use these structures to grow tomatoes, peppers, and squash.

A mini-greenhouse can be built with recycled or reject lengths of lumber. With the raised bed as base and foundation, it is easy to add six vertical supports cut into 1.2-metre (4-foot) lengths. We insert these verticals into the soil in the corners and middle of the bed, fastening them in place by screwing through the sides of the bed. Two- to 3-metre (8- or 10-foot) stringers of wood (2-by-3s are ideal for this) are used to create horizontal beams attached to the tops of the vertical supports along the sides of the bed. On top of these rails, we install triangular frames to support a ridge beam. This creates a little house that can then be covered with rolled plastic.

We staple plastic to the frame at both ends of the structure. The top is covered with a roll of plastic, stapled down on the upwind side of the raised bed, and secured with strapping screwed down over the edge of the plastic. The downwind side of the plastic is loose but needs added weight, so we sandwich that edge between two lengths of 2- by 3-inch (5- by 7.5-centimetre) lumber, screwed together, to make it easy to roll up the plastic on a sunny day or when access to the bed is needed.

These forms of protection create microenvironments that will protect garden plants from wind and cold. Designing and building these structures saves time later, as they help you deal with the challenges of seasonal weather. With these methods, you can extend the growing season by up to two months. Protective structures allow you to move plants out weeks earlier during the spring and leave them in the ground later in the fall.

12. THE GREENHOUSE

Greenhouse design. A greenhouse is a full-sized walk-in structure with transparent walls, heated by the sun that provides a sheltered grow space, to allow production in colder months. As with the other shelter structures already described, the goal of a greenhouse is to block wind and capture warmth. The greenhouse creates a microclimate that relies on the sun as its main heating source, which means that during warm months significant venting is needed to shed heat and humidity, even though during the colder winter months and the shoulder seasons of spring and fall, the challenge is to capture and retain more heat to create ideal growing conditions.

We have learned to build unheated passive solar structures using primarily recycled materials. Additional supplies needed for a 10-square-metre (100-square-foot) greenhouse can be sourced for a few hundred dollars. With walls of recycled glass and polycarbonate panels for the roof, framed with wood recycled from other buildings, we have built greenhouses onto the side of our own backyard shed and a neighbour's barn at a basic cost less than $300.

For the northern gardener, the standard glasshouse design inherited from Europe—a building with transparent roof and walls—is not suitable. With the greenhouse's long dimension running east to west, the north wall and roof become a major heat-loss zone, even if some reflected northern light is coming in. We advocate a northern greenhouse with a fully insulated north-facing wall and roof to retain heat.

Friends and neighbours who have tested this idea have found that it works really well. For David Goodyear's earth-sheltered four-season greenhouse at The Homestead in Flatrock, the greenhouse design includes an insulated concrete back wall sunk into the side of a south-facing hill. The concrete in the wall absorbs and stores sun energy so effectively that only a small amount of additional heat is needed even in the depths of winter. In Goodyear's design, heat is stored underground using a GAHT (Ground Air Heat Transfer) system: a small fan forces air from the top of the building through a 6-inch tube and down through underground channels where heat and moisture are stored in the soil beneath the building. Then, when

    DAN RUBIN

you need to add warmth to the greenhouse, the same 1.5-horsepower fan pulls warm air up from where it has been stored.

Greenhouses can be framed in wood or metal and are most effective when their longest dimension runs east to west. This orientation provides a long south-facing wall that can be sheathed in glass or plastic to enable sunlight to penetrate into the greenhouse interior. We have used recycled window units (the larger and more uniform in size, the better) to create two inexpensive home-built greenhouses, but if recycled windows are not available, we recommend flat sheets of laminated polycarbonate that have durability, strength, and some insulation value for the transparent surfaces of the structure. These are excellent materials for the south-facing walls and greenhouse roof.

The east and west walls, depending on the site, are a suitable place to install vents and windows but should be insulated to increase winter heat retention. A well-insulated north wall and roof hold in the sun energy that enters the building from the south, retaining heat during winter, when the sun is low in the sky.

Another major consideration for greenhouse design is size. The smaller the greenhouse, the less work you can do inside it. There is a significant difference between a greenhouse 2 metres (6 feet), 2.5 metres (8 feet), 4 metres (12 feet), or 4.5 metres (14 feet) wide in terms of how you can actually use the structure. In general, cost per square metre drops as size increases. You can spend up to $100 per square metre for a kit and double that if you

David Goodyear's four-season greenhouse is a passive solar structure equipped with an underground heat storage system.

pay someone to build and install the greenhouse. Working with recycled materials, or building a wooden frame, covered with a roll of 6 mil plastic will, of course, be much cheaper. For only a little more, you can purchase greenhouse plastic that has been treated to resist degradation in UV light.

Whether the structure is free-standing (firmly anchored to the ground) or built against the side of an existing building, with basic ingenuity, careful design, and bracing for structural strength you can create a simple home greenhouse that offers protection from wind and cold.

Anyone with strong intention and basic tools can build a greenhouse. Just remember: venting air and moisture is critical to plant health in the warmer months. Because heat rises, an intake

DAN RUBIN

port low in one end wall and an exhaust vent (equipped with a fan) high in the other end wall, or in the roof, is essential. In winter, heating can extend the use of a greenhouse through the coldest months. Heating options include electrical baseboard elements, a heater with a fan, heat generated by a compost pile, or heated water from a stove or furnace, circulated through the soil.

This chapter has provided a brief overview of greenhouse design and operation. For further details, we recommend these books published by New Society Publishers, based on Gabriola Island, British Columbia: *The Year-Round Solar Greenhouse* by Lindsey Schiller and Mark Plinke; and *The Chinese Greenhouse: Design and Build a Low-Cost PassiveSolar Greenhouse*, both by Dan Chiras. These books include detailed designs for passive solar structures that can extend the growing season in northern locations.

If you are looking for an existing greenhouse design, check with friends who have built their own or study online plans or those in the recommended books.

Three construction options. To create a greenhouse, you can purchase a kit, have a local contractor build it, or design and build one yourself using available materials. The key in each of these approaches is to carefully consider the quality and stability of the structure before you commit to it. In the case of manufactured

The earth-sheltered greenhouse combines the design of a greenhouse and a root cellar and can be built with standard construction materials.

kits, cost and ability to withstand strong winds are key considerations. When hiring a contractor, visit a structure that he or she has built to assess its effectiveness and aesthetics. Unless the prospective builder knows how to create a sturdy, well-built greenhouse, you may be better off doing the work yourself or finding a carpenter who can follow a greenhouse plan. The builder must understand that standard roof trusses do not work well in a greenhouse because they block out too much light coming in through the roof and restrict usable space for vertical growing and that, unlike a standard shed or garage, venting is essential to effective operation in warm months.

The earth-sheltered greenhouse under construction in 2022 at the O'Brien Farm in St. John's is part of a series of experiments being carried out across Newfoundland and Labrador to find ways to extend the growing season without burning fossil fuels to heat a greenhouse.

     DAN RUBIN

Proper greenhouse design includes good structural strength, solid anchoring to resist wind shear, while orienting the long dimension of the greenhouse east to west to maximize sun entry from the south. Regardless of size and construction materials, the structure's location is critical. The farther you have to walk to reach your greenhouse, the less likely you will be to use it for year-round production. If you plan to grow only in warm months, this is not as important. Finally, consider how nearby trees and other buildings will shade the structure as they grow over time!

Greenhouse operation. The basic process of managing a greenhouse involves regulating temperature and humidity to create optimum growing conditions inside the structure, while providing rich soil and an appropriate supply of water for irrigation. These sheltered grow spaces also create inviting conditions for a range of pests and pathogens, including mould. Climate control inside a greenhouse is a trade-off because you need to provide warmth and moisture while limiting these negative impacts.

Air movement into and through the structure is the key, particularly during the warm, moist months of late spring, summer, and early fall. Proper location of vents and use of fans to move air inside and through the structure can prevent the buildup of moisture and mould, as well as distributing fresh carbon dioxide and warmth

to prevent these from becoming trapped in the structure's peak. Inexpensive automatic hydraulic vent openers are recommended for venting control.

The goal during colder months is to maintain a minimum level of warmth. Not every plant needs a lot of heat to flourish. Cold-tolerant greens may be planted in the fall; with the right conditions, they can be harvested all through the winter. Plants suitable for low-temperature greenhouse propagation include lettuce, arugula, spinach, chard, white turnips, Red Giant mustard, bok choy, feng qing choy, and corn salad. These plants thrive in temperatures as low as 4° to 5°C and can be harvested as they mature or planted in trays for repeated cutting as microgreens.

A greenhouse with minimal winter heating and a well-insulated north wall and roof, equipped with some form of thermal mass (material with the capacity to retain heat) such as a concrete wall or water held in barrels, requires only a small amount of additional heat to maintain the 4° or 5°C needed for winter greens. As spring arrives, the sun moves higher in the sky and more

 DAN RUBIN

TEMPERATURES FOR SEED GERMINATION

(All temperatures given in Celsius)

Crop	Minimum temperature	Optimum temperature	Maximum temperature
Asparagus	10	24-30	35
Beans	15.5	24- 0	30
Beets	4.5	18-30	35
Broccoli	4.5	15-30	35
Cabbage	4.5	15-30	35
Carrots	4.5	18-30	35
Cauliflower	4.5	18- 30	35
Celery	4.5	21 (night)/30 (day)	30
Chard	4.5	18-30	35
Corn	10	18-35	40
Cucumber	15.5	18-35	40
Eggplant	15.5	24-30	35
Garlic	0	18-30	35
Leek	0	18-30	35
Lettuce	0	15-24	30
Melons	15.5	24-30	40
Onions	0	18-30	35
Parsley	4.5	18-30	35
Parsnips	0	18-24	35
Peas	4.5	18-24	30
Pepper	15.5	18-24	35
Pumpkin	15.5	30-35	40
Radish	4.5	18-30	35
Spinach	0	18-24	24
Squash	15.5	30-35	40
Tomato	10	18-30	35
Turnip	4.5	15-35	40

Each species of garden vegetable has a minimum temperature needed for seed germination.

* With thanks to the University of California Extension Service for this data.

sun energy is gradually delivered, so then the challenge becomes cooling the building to maintain an ideal grow space.

During the darker, colder months, lights in the greenhouse will allow you to see what you are doing and provide a supplementary source of heat. Adding grow lights increases the number of hours of light a plant receives each day and can turn the greenhouse into an area for spring seed starting. The chart on page 121 shows minimum germination temperatures for various food plants and flowers; some plants can be started earlier in colder surroundings, some later, depending on the temperature they need for germination and time before they are planted out into the greenhouse or garden.

     DAN RUBIN

Under the full glare of the summer sun, greenhouse operation becomes an exercise in cooling and moving air through the structure, while keeping out unwanted insects. Screening the intake and exhaust vents is desirable, as long as the pollinators needed to produce fruit are not screened out. Automatic sensors and thermostats available from garden supply centres and online sellers allow for automatic monitoring and recording of variations in temperature and can help you prevent overheating.

Regulating temperature is essential. Opening and closing doors and vents is an ongoing effort, crucial for maintaining optimal growing conditions, protecting plants from cold and frost in spring and fall while allowing excess heat to escape during summer days. We have installed a recording thermometer in our greenhouse, that broadcasts to a unit in our kitchen giving us current temperatures, along with the daily maximum and minimum. This affordable unit allows you to steadily monitor greenhouse growing conditions.

For most greenhouses, even small backyard structures, a fan to exhaust heat and humid air is needed during warm months. Large industrial fans designed for use in commercial greenhouses are expensive and noisy; unless you have a large greenhouse, buy a standard household fan and mount it on a shelf just inside the exhaust vent. This fan can be equipped with a timer or temperature sensor.

If you grow in raised beds or containers inside a greenhouse, an additional challenge is to maintain soil fertility. By replacing the soil every year or every other year or by adding compost, manure, and fertilizer, the growing medium can be kept from being stripped of key nutrients. Supplying beds and containers with fresh, organic-rich soil is essential in the greenhouse, just as it is in outdoor garden beds. Both major nutrients (nitrogen, phosphorus, and potassium) and the various micronutrients that can limit plant growth need to be added each year.

     DAN RUBIN

Although commercial greenhouses, especially high-tech structures operating in the Netherlands, use complicated grow systems with plants attached to tracks or netting, effective vertical use of space in a home greenhouse can be achieved by simply hanging plants overhead to make better use of available warm space.

From herbs in containers to squash and tomatoes planted in boxes and beds, a wide range of food can be grown on platforms or hung, with their vines or branches hanging down. Vine-forming plants such as indeterminate tomatoes, squash, cucumbers, and beans can be trained to grow vertically, supported by wires or strings, as long as they do not create a screen along the south wall that shades the other plants.

Plan your greenhouse space to maximize light for all plants. As you develop a design, keep in mind that different plants grow to different heights to create a constantly evolving seasonal landscape inside the greenhouse. Our small greenhouse is transformed each year from an overwintering space for protecting dormant plants into a space for seed starting and hardening off, then becomes a vertical grow space with hanging plants, plants in the ground, and plants on shelves, filling the interior space at the peak of the growing season.

The author's greenhouse, reframed with cedar, will last at least another decade. Post-and-beam construction makes this possible, because the roof is supported by 6- by-6-inch posts in the outer corners, resting on a concrete foundation.

13. CONTAINER GARDENING

Another useful strategy for northern gardeners is to grow food and flowers in containers that can range from ceramic or plastic plant pots to recycled bins, barrels, boxes, drawers, and bathtubs. Recycled bathtubs, particularly old-fashioned claw-foot tubs, can become a solid, large, and durable space for growing, once they are filled with rich soil.

Strawberries respond particularly well to being grown in containers and some tomatoes, especially the determinate, bush varieties, are ideal for container gardening. In summer, our back deck, facing the open Atlantic, is lined with an assortment of glazed pots in various sizes in which we raise tomatoes, geraniums, and other flowering plants.

Container growing requires attention to two basic plant needs: adequate drainage and rich soil. Because the soil within each container is limited and can become exhausted, it should be replaced every year or two. Growing in containers is therefore a bit more work than growing directly in the garden or in raised beds. The soil discarded

from containers in the fall can be used to add tilth to garden beds or can join the compost bin. Good drainage requires loose soil and multiple holes in the bottom of a container. Avoid overwatering; waterlogged soil can cause roots at the bottom to rot and die.

Containers. Choices for containers include plant pots in a full range of sizes, from small clay pots to glazed ceramic planters to the lightweight plastic versions made to look as if they were ceramic (that are much lighter and easier to move and store). A wide range of recycled receptacles from wooden boxes to waste baskets, from shipping crates to water carriers, can be turned into plant pots by drilling drainage holes in their bottoms. A favourite option, here in the land of cod, is the fish box, a large, heavy rectangular plastic container with handles at each end, used for transporting fish.

Drainage. Multiple drain holes ensure that standing water does not collect in the bottom of a planter. Avoid placing loose materials in the bottom. To our surprise, we recently learned that the spaces between gravel or other gritty material block water flow, because the surface tension in those small spaces creates air pockets, through

    DAN RUBIN

which water cannot flow. Fill containers with a good-quality potting mix or garden soil mixed with sand, with only small bits of shell, broken crockery, or plastic at the bottom to keep soil from escaping through the drainage holes. Once planted, we place the containers on a wooden frame on the deck so that their wet bottoms do not sit directly on the deck boards and cause rot.

Planting. Because containers warm up quickly in the sun, they are ideal for early planting and season extension. In the spring and late fall, when temperatures occasionally fall below 0°C, the soil in a large pot will insulate the plant's roots. Planting out flowers and herbs that have overwintered indoors extends the growing season because these plants are more cold-hardy, while seeds sown directly into containers need a week or more to germinate before they sprout. Just as in your garden, mulching the surface of the soil retains warmth and moisture.

Make sure that the bedding plants you purchase are healthy, vigorous, and free of aphids and other pests before setting them out in containers. You can plant more than one type of herb or vegetable in each pot. With large-stemmed plants, such as tomatoes, only a single plant goes in a planter, because the tomato plant will develop a dense root system and can use up the nutrients in the pot. But you can plant two, three, or even four of your favourite herbs in a single large pot, and place it just outside the kitchen door, where they will be easy to harvest when needed for cooking.

Watering. One lesson for happy container gardening is to avoid overwatering. If plants droop, they may need water, but otherwise intermittent watering is best. Following a weekly watering schedule can help. Rainfall is a consideration, but weekly watering helps you gauge the amount of water your plants need. And why not feed as you water? Use diluted fertilizer, particularly fish and seaweed emulsions, to add micronutrients along with nitrogen, phosphorus, and potassium to support growth, flowering, and fruiting.

Planting in buckets. Some local gardeners have built a potato ladder—a stepped wooden frame holding 20-litre (5-gallon) buckets to grow potatoes, carrots, and other vegetables. While some have had success (if they use rich soil and space out what they plant), others, with poor-quality garden soil and overcrowded buckets, have not found this method to be very effective.

Rich organic soil and effective drainage are keys to success with container gardening. In a 20-litre (5-gallon) bucket, you can plant a dozen carrots, but crowding results in thinner carrots. Our

     DAN RUBIN

passion for container gardening is well satisfied by the flowers, tomatoes, and herbs growing on our deck—but we also have a large backyard garden. If you have room for raised beds in your backyard, or a lawn waiting to be turned into a vegetable garden, plant there. But for those who have a more restricted space for gardening, or none at all, growing in buckets or building a potato ladder can convert unused space into food production capacity.

Citrus. Some indoor gardeners are having success with lemons, oranges, mandarins, and kumquats grown in containers, protected through winter and spring in a sunroom or south-facing heated porch with good winter sun, then moved outdoors in the warmer months. This practice stretches back to Italian, Dutch, and French orangeries that were built to grow citrus in the 1600s. Another exotic plant that fascinated European gardeners was the Caribbean pineapple. Pineapples became a sign of wealth and prestige after they were imported to be grown inside pineries by wealthy estate owners in England and Scotland.

Houseplants. Growing plants indoors, with or without lights, can become a wonderful part of your garden year. Succulents and semi-tropical plants, such as aloe (used to treat burns) and the decorative jade tree, which can grow well over 1 metre (3 feet) tall, are among the dozens of plants from tropical and semi-tropical climates that will grow in containers inside our homes. Container gardening can bring parts of the garden indoors and keep them growing all winter.

14. EXTENDING THE GROWING SEASON

The northern gardener's general goal is to extend the growing season, to give plants more time to grow and produce food or flowers, despite the short season of warm summer weather. Multiple strategies and techniques help achieve this.

Seed starting. During the winter months, before the garden year begins, we plan what we will grow. We order seeds early in the new year and decide when to start them, based on each variety's rate of germination and cold tolerance. The most cold-tolerant are planted first, because they can go outdoors sooner. Sprouted under lights in a warm indoor location, and then potted on into larger containers, they get a head start on the growing year.

We prepare our basement grow space by hanging two levels of lighting fixtures above a table where the seeds are started. A second shelf is below the top level of lights. Strong light is required to support the plants' initial growth. This simple, inexpensive seed-starting setup uses full-spectrum (daylight) fluorescent tubes in fixtures hung on chains, so that the light can be placed as close to the plant pots

Grow lights allow an early start for vegetables, herbs, and flowers.

as possible. Providing sufficient light intensity as well as warmth is essential to keep young plants from becoming "leggy" (long and thin) as they reach for the light. Our light fixtures are hung on chains and can be gradually raised as the plants grow taller.

Debate continues about light efficiency, colour selection, and the use of LEDs to deliver higher light intensity with less power consumption, but standard fluorescent tubes do provide enough light for seed starting, if they are full-spectrum, daylight tubes.

LED lights reduce power cost and provide more illumination for seed starting, and then it is not as necessary to place lights directly on top of the young plants. On the downside, LEDs require a larger initial investment and replacement units are costly. They do not generate the same level of heat as fluorescent tubes do. Heat is useful for seed starting, although excess heat can dry out the soil and burn foliage.

While various recycled containers can be used for seed starting—if they have drainage holes in the bottom—we generally rely on standard 10-centimetre (4-inch) plastic pots that can be washed, sterilized in a mild bleach solution, and re-used. We can fit nine of these plant pots into each square foot of space. We can plant up to four seeds in each pot, to maximize space used for initial germination. If all the seeds in a container sprout, they will need to be separated and potted on into larger plant pots when they are 5 to 8 centimetres (2 to 3 inches) tall. Multiple seeding allows more plants to be started under the same lights, in a small space.

Some gardeners use peat pods, recycled egg cartons, and other tiny containers for more efficient use of space and because they are cheap. Peat pods consist of dried peat encased in plastic mesh; they expand after the pods are watered, but their small size can cause problems. Each pod is wrapped in a layer of plastic mesh which must be either stripped and discarded or buried in the soil. We caution against using these containers: they are too small to allow for healthy root growth once the seed sprouts.

Hardening off. If plants are moved suddenly to colder outdoor settings, they can go into shock. Bright sun can also slow their growth, cause bleaching, or kill them. The process of gradually moving plants out of the protected space where the seeds were started to outdoor conditions is called hardening off, a gradual process of adapting to lower temperatures.

In our small backyard greenhouse, this process is straightforward: we erect a long bench in the sunny, southeast-facing windows as a place to acclimatize plants to the cold. Because the plants inside the greenhouse are protected from wind and extreme ranges of temperature, this is an ideal location for hardening off. If you do not have a greenhouse, a recommended structure for hardening off is a cold frame or a small cloche with a window or hinged lid.

You can also harden off young bedding plants by moving them outdoors to a sheltered, sunny deck or your yard on a warm day, bringing them back in at night for several consecutive days. In this way, the more gradual transition to outdoors helps plants adapt to the new conditions.

     DAN RUBIN

Another way to harden off is to plant the seedlings outdoors, then cover them with a tent of floating row cover for protection from wind and cold. Regardless of whether you harden off plants in a covered raised bed, a cold frame, or a greenhouse, hardening off prepares the bedding plants for their move to the garden.

Protective structures. In chapter 11, we described how to build protective structures from rock, straw bales, lumber, plastic, or glass. Whether your garden design is crude and built from recycled materials, or neat as a pin, building or purchasing enclosures can protect plants from wind, cold, and insect pests. This can extend the growing season by up to two months.

Succession planting. Planting successive rows of the same plant in the same bed week by week is called interplanting or succession planting. Succession planting creates a continuous flow of harvestable food through the growing season. Leafy greens such as lettuce, spinach, chard, kale, arugula, and Chinese greens are especially appropriate for this. As the weather warms, these species tend to bolt (produce flowers and go to seed), but this is not a problem if you have done a second planting to create a fresh cycle of the same plant.

Succession planting works best if you keep track of when it is time to plant again. A garden calendar or journal helps you schedule replanting. Fast-growing vegetables can be planted roughly every two weeks to create repeated harvests of leafy greens. Warm weather crops that take longer to mature, such as tomatoes or squash, need to be in the ground earlier and may not be appropriate for multiple plantings in a cold climate with a short growing season.

Late harvest. With some form of protection in place, you can wait to harvest or, in some cases, leave crops in the ground for a winter harvest. We know folks who leave potatoes, onions, leeks, kale, parsnips, carrots, and winter greens in place for a late fall and winter harvest. Protecting the soil with a thick mulch deters frost from entering the ground, making it easier to dig.

Seed saving. Another type of late harvest is the fall seed harvest. In October and November, poppies and other garden flowers produce mature seed heads that we harvest and dry to save seed for replanting the following year(s). Biennials such as kale take two years to go to seed. Kale's bright golden flowers become thin, sickle-shaped seed pods which eventually dry and turn brown. We harvest the pods as they start to pop open and dry them indoors. We shuck seeds from the pods once they are fully dried, then clean and continue to dry the seeds, which we sell through our company website and use for replanting in our own garden. You can harvest seed for replanting in the same way.

     DAN RUBIN

Curing your crop. Winter squash can be left on the vine to mature and harden, to prepare for winter storage. Cucurbits and root vegetables such as potatoes, onions, and garlic must be cured in order to store well. Curing is a process of drying in warm air. Laying the harvest out in the garden on a raised screen or on a wooden deck in the full sun also works well. With warm air circulating around all sides, these vegetables develop a hard exterior and become more dependable for winter storage. Without curing them, it is more likely that mould spores will cause the food you have grown to be lost. Do not wash root vegetables before storage. Doing so can introduce mould spores into onions, garlic, and other vegetables. It is better to dry them and brush off any remaining dirt without getting them wet.

Extending the growing season depends on a collection of strategies, from starting seeds indoors to hardening them off and planting into the garden in raised beds equipped with protective structures to keep plants warm and protect them from wind and cold, allowing for a later harvest and overwintering some crops.

15. PESTS AND PLANT DISEASES

Wherever you garden, you will encounter pests and plant diseases. Depending on weather conditions, the location of your garden, and the surrounding landscape, you will likely have to deal with one or more of these common garden threats.

Resist the urge to jump up and down muttering "kill, kill, kill" when you discover that something has been eating your plants. We have adopted the notion that humans are in charge of the world and that anything that decreases or threatens the maximum yield of food must be eradicated. This is a fundamental mistake. We are not in charge and never have been. Our goal should be to become better partners with nature, using what we learn to restore balance. Healthy plants are less likely to support pests and succumb to disease. That does not mean that there is nothing we can do when we see evidence of imbalance. Here are common culprits and recommendations for how to deal with them appropriately.

Slugs and snails. Living in a wet, cold northern climate—whether in the rainforests of British Columbia, along the rocky shorelines of the east coast, or in the evergreen forests of the north—gardeners have to deal with these gastropod molluscs that slither through our gardens, leaving trails of slime behind them. While we may not appreciate slugs and snails, they are a necessary part of the natural ecosystem; as decomposers, they play an important role in breaking down dead and decaying plant material. Without them, and the fungi, bacteria, and worms that also provide this service, we would be up to our eyeballs in plant debris in just a few years. When they enter our gardens, slugs and snails find fresh leafy material for their diet. Every gardener will have their own way of dealing with this problem. In our garden, we avoid all commercial pesticides: we do not want to use those poisons anywhere near our growing food.

Even so, we do not like it when slugs or snails munch on our plants. The most effective way of limiting their damage is the evening slug hunt: go out with a flashlight and container and remove or kill slugs using salt, scissors, or a container of warm beer to drown them. Making this a family activity can be rewarding, if your family members are not too squeamish about slaughtering the slippery invaders.

A second approach is to top-dress the beds with wood chips, diatomaceous earth, or another material that slugs and snails avoid

in their movement through the garden. These coarse materials wash away in the rain. Some gardeners swear by this approach, but we have had mixed success discouraging slugs with coarse material in our garden beds. A third way involves protecting the edges of a raised bed with a thin strip of copper wire or flat copper strips sold in garden supply stores. We have no convincing evidence that slugs and snails will not cross a copper strip; some gardeners have reported that copper strips do not stop snails and slugs. But others (and the product manufacturers) claim that they do.

Another deterrent to slug and snail activity was recommended to us by a fellow gardener here in Newfoundland. He surrounds his garden beds with a row of potato plants; he believes that slugs and snails are repelled by the odour of the potato leaves.

Finally, the beer trap: a bowl or can of beer sunk into the soil becomes an inviting target for slugs, who drown themselves in the alcohol. However, evaporation and rain will require regular recharging of the container, and how much beer do you donate to slugs?

Commercial poisons in the form of slug bait are also available, but use these with care, since the bait can also be ingested by pets and small children. The Safer brand slug baits are organic and non-toxic to birds, dogs, and cats. If properly placed and weighted down, slug bait diminishes the amount of predation on plants but may not totally solve the problem.

Slugs hide during the day and come out at night. This means that they need a shelter. Favourite hangouts are underneath planks, in thick leaves and other mulch materials, and in crevices in rock walls. Looking for them in these places and eliminating their hiding places is a good strategy.

We respect slugs and snails as a natural part of the garden. But because we do not want them to damage our crops, we create sacrifice zones with plantings that we allow them to consume. Kale and other leafy greens can serve as sacrificial crops.

Clearing a space around beds and mulching with a thick carpet of wood chips makes the area less attractive for slugs and snails.

Insect pests. Each plant species has co-evolved with the insects that have become specialized to pollinate them or ingest their leaves. This activity is part of maintaining a natural balance. One mistake in industrial food production is planting large areas in monocultures of exactly the same variety of plant. This invites insects to a feast. They thrive when there is so much of the same food in one place, and spread out from there. By planting a varied garden, including plants that repel pests (chrysanthemum, calendula, lavender, petunia, basil, thyme, mint, chives, mosquito plant, and chervil), you can protect your garden from insect pests.

If you plant tomatoes, watch closely for the large, striped green "tomato worm." Remove them by hand.

Flea beetles, whitefly, carrot rust fly, and cabbage butterfly caterpillars may appear, depending on the crop. Because flying insects lay their eggs on certain target plants (rust fly on carrots, cabbage butterfly on brassicas), you can protect your plants with a layer of screen or floating row cover to prevent egg deposit.

We build frames over our raised beds, drape floating row cover over hoops, and seal the edges by stapling the fabric down or weighing it down along the edges with heavy lumber. The key:

DAN RUBIN

there must be no gaps in your coverage.

Whitefly. These tiny, white flying insects damage plants in the greenhouse or outdoors and are difficult to control. Although some gardeners use insecticides, biological poisons can also wipe out beneficial insects. A solution of 15 millilitres (1 tablespoon) of liquid dish soap in 4 litres (1 gallon) of water sprayed on the plants should kill adult whiteflies without harming plant growth.

Aphids. Aphids are mostly often found in greenhouses, but sometimes they appear outdoors in a moist garden bed. These tiny light green insects are remarkable survivors that travel from garden to garden on transplants. Check purchased bedding plants carefully for any sign of aphids on leaf undersides. Once they have infested the greenhouse, they are hard to get rid of. But with persistence, they can be removed by washing plants with a strong spray of water outside the greenhouse, and then spraying a mixture of garlic oil, cayenne powder, and water on the leaves every three or four days until all sign of aphids has been eliminated.

Ontario permaculture orchardist Stephen Sobkowiak told us that "aphids are a message." What is the message? "Too much nitrogen in the soil. They feed on the sap within the leaves and are always looking for the sugars that the plant produces." If you are confronted by aphids, consider reducing the nitrogen fertilizers in the plant soil used in your greenhouse.

Spider mites. These tiny critters appear as red, yellow, or brown patches on leaf undersides. They are not insects, but miniature members of the arachnid family, along with spiders, ticks, and scorpions. Because they are smaller than the head of a pin, they are difficult to identify. Spider mites often appear in greenhouses, where warmth and humidity encourage their spread. After they mature, they weave soft webs and reproduce. They damage leaves, creating brown spots where they have fed. Once spider mites have been identified (shake them onto white paper for confirmation), spray the plants with water to remove them or bring in ladybugs or other natural predators. An application of dormant oil on trees in the spring also limits their spread.

Scale. These sap-sucking insects appear as small black or brown scaly patches on stems and leaf undersides. They are a particular problem on fruit trees and some flowering shrubs. Remove them by hand or, more effectively, apply dormant oil in early spring to the entire tree. This non-toxic oil coats any existing scale and suffocates them. Scale lives on the leaves, extracting sap and exuding tiny bubbles of a sugary liquid called honeydew. Ants are attracted to, and feed on, honeydew, so their presence on trees may indicate that scale is present. Mealy bugs, a larger insect pest, can also be dealt with by applying horticultural dormant oil.

     DAN RUBIN

Cabbage worm. Small green or brown caterpillars emerge from eggs deposited by the cabbage white butterfly (not a moth) on leaves of plants in the cabbage family. The cabbage worm can devastate a head of cabbage, munching on the tender leaves and leaving mushy brown droppings. They attack all members of the brassica family once their eggs have been laid. The best way to protect plants, other than by hunting and removing the green caterpillars, is to enclose them with floating row cover or a screen to prevent egg deposition.

Rust fly. Rust fly larvae burrow into the roots of carrots, turnips, and other root crops, leaving dark lines that turn them bitter and useless as food. We grew carrots in fresh soil successfully our first two years. But in the third year, rust fly appeared. We knew it had laid eggs in the soil and would stay active for some time. After letting the bed rest a few years, we again planted and harvested carrots. We place a door screen over the bed to act as a lid and prevent the carrot rust fly from entering. Our recommendation for rust fly is the same as for the cabbage white butterfly: keep them from laying eggs by screening off the areas where you grow root crops. A wall or screen around the beds, at least 45 centimetres (1.5 feet) above the soil, will keep most low-flying insects from reaching the plants.

Cutworms. These chunky, inch-long "worms" are actually caterpillars that turn into moths. Cutworms live in the soil and emerge at night to chew through the base of the stem of various flowers and vegetable plants. Although they are easy to see and pick off, you can also deter them by placing collars of cardboard around the base of the plants. Cutworms are common in early

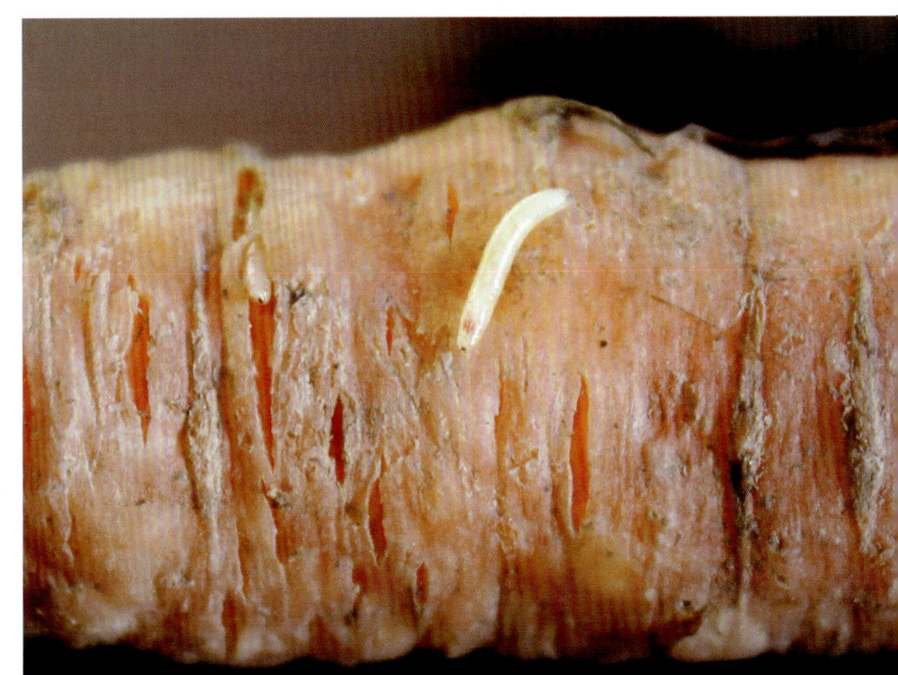

summer; they do not appear as frequently if a long, hard winter has kept them under control.

Beetles. Various types of beetles specific to particular plants, including Colorado potato beetles, Mexican bean beetles, click beetles (the larval forms are known as wireworms), flea beetles, and invasive Japanese beetles, have become major concerns among commercial growers in warmer climates. They are less common in the north. If they do appear, and after positive identification (do not kill ladybugs and other beetles that are beneficial predators), use floating row cover and spray with insecticidal soaps to limit their spread or eliminate them.

Leaf miners. These invasive insects insert themselves into the insides of leaves, turning the areas they inhabit white and semi-transparent. They frequent kale and chard, among other plants. Leaf miners are annoying, but rarely kill the plants that they invade. Removing infested leaves is the best approach. You can also spray plants with neem oil or a solution made with hot peppers, till the soil to kill or remove insect eggs, and use floating row cover to keep them away. If you wait until fall and remove infested leaf parts, you limit their damage.

Earwigs. Although some gardeners have serious concerns about earwigs in their garden, we see them as a natural part of the soil ecology and, except for strawberries, have seen little or no damage done by them in 20 years. But if there are too many earwigs in your beds, and if you do confirm that they are damaging crops, consider decreasing the amount of nitrogen-rich fertilizer added to the beds to restrict their main source of food. A mixture of rubbing alcohol and water, which evaporates once it is sprayed on the leaves, is another way to deal with earwigs. Dish soap solutions also repel earwigs. Some gardeners install traps of canola or olive oil, sunk in the ground, to attract and drown them. Boric acid powder can be

     DAN RUBIN

lightly sprinkled on the ground; but excessive amounts poison the soil and deter future plant growth. As with any population, it may take a while for predators to arrive to control earwigs, but in time the predators will come.

Mould and mildew. These fungal infestations signal high levels of moisture in a garden or greenhouse, likely resulting from overwatering, watering late in the day, or a combination of warmth and moisture. Reducing the conditions that promote mildew will address this condition.

Black spot. A fungal disease, common on roses but also found on Norway maple, black spot appears as black patches spreading across leaves and is encouraged by warm, wet growing conditions. While it may be unsightly, it does not normally damage plants.

Black knot. A fungal disease, spread by spores, black knot infects plum, cherry, and other stone fruit trees on the east coast of Canada, causing gnarled, thick, black to brown growths to appear on tree limbs. Prune out all signs of black knot, along with the associated limb, to prevent its spread. Black-knot-diseased wood should not be buried or burned, as that can spread the disease. Cut up the branches and discard them in the trash. After cutting out black knot, or any other diseased part of a plant, sterilize your tools with a strong bleach solution to kill any remaining spores.

Fire blight. Browning and withering of apple, pear, dogberry (rowan) leaves, and other trees can be a sign of fire blight, a disease that has seriously impacted orchards across North America. We have lost two dogberries to this bacterial disease and have become aware of the importance of not passing it from tree to tree. Sterilize tools after each use with bleach solution. Removing infected leaves and branches helps, but once the bacterium infests a tree, it may be too late to save it. Fire blight, however, does not stay in the soil; if the tree dies or must be removed, it is safe to plant in the same area the following year. Fire blight enters trees through flowers and wounds created by pruning. Sealing cuts with wax or bitumen is recommended when pruning fruit trees.

Tobacco mosaic virus. Although named for the tobacco plants which are its primary host, the mosaic virus also attacks tomatoes and other nightshades, causing mottled yellow and green leaves that curl over, reducing yield. No chemical controls exist for this viral condition, which attacks tomatoes, peppers, potatoes, apples, pears, and cherries, while a related version affects cucumbers, lettuce, beets, petunias, and, naturally, tobacco. Since the virus is common in its primary host, tobacco, keep smokers away from plants because they can transmit the virus by hand or in cigarette smoke. Isolating plants is the best way to prevent mosaic virus spread.

Damping off. A fungal disease that affects young plants, especially bedding plants in early stages of growth, damping off causes bedding plants to droop and die. There is no known treatment for this once it begins. You must replant. Damping off happens when unsterilized soil is used for seed starting or when too much water has been applied to young plants. To prevent damping off, use properly sterilized potting mix, avoid overwatering, and ensure adequate air movement around new plants.

Fusarium. A common soil-borne fungus, fusarium causes plants such as strawberries, tomatoes, beans, peas, and asparagus to wilt and become stunted as their stems turn black. If fusarium appears, remove and destroy affected plants and avoid planting the same species in the same spot for up to five years. There is no known chemical treatment for fusarium for home gardeners.

Rust. This large group of fungal diseases causes rusty spots on leaves. The spots often have a red-orange colour that turns brown to black, then the leaf dies. Rusts occur in hollyhocks, daylilies, tomatoes, and especially roses. Commercial fungicides are available,

     DAN RUBIN

but it is best to remove and destroy, or bag and discard, any affected leaves and stems to keep the fungus from overwintering and persisting into the following year.

Many in our society assume that poisons can maintain control by eliminating pests and treat plant diseases, as though they could be eliminated, killed, or stamped out. This view demonizes functional parts of the natural world.

When we apply biocides (biological poisons) to kill pests, we obtain temporary relief, but all that is accomplished is to make the "pests" stronger, enabling pesticide producers to sell even more product. The smaller the virus, bacterium, or insect, the more quickly it will reproduce and so, generation after generation, it adapts to whatever chemical is being used, and we end up using more and more poisons.

In moving away from industrial agriculture and toward a more sustainable and regenerative approach to food production, farmers are realizing that their goal is not to control nature but to create balance. As we regenerate rich, healthy soils, and return organic materials to the earth, we restore the grand cycles of return on which nature depends, to create healthy soil and grow healthy food. Plants can then resist disease, and by growing more varied crops, we mimic the natural world and keep pests at bay.

For the home gardener, avoiding pesticides, herbicides, and chemical fertilizers is essential to growing healthy food. A growing body of evidence supports no-dig, permaculture, biodynamic gardening, and regenerative agriculture. These approaches have many benefits over trying to control a garden with deep cultivation, poisonous sprays, and soil amendments that arrive by the bag from somewhere far away. If you do your own research into permaculture and regenerative agriculture, you will find more and more ways to make your garden healthier and your work in it easier.

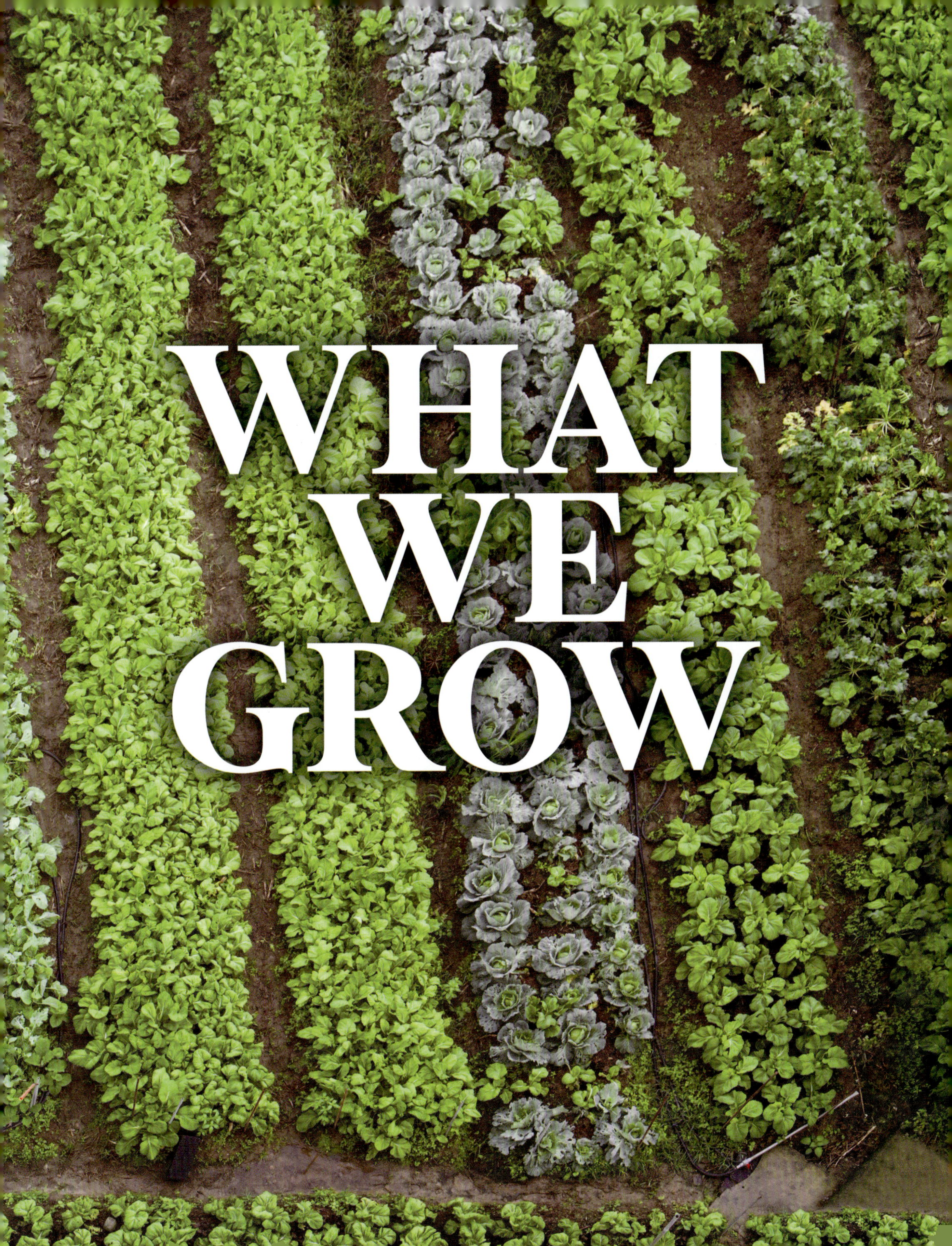

WHAT
WE
GROW

15. SALAD GREENS

Familiar greens such as lettuce, spinach, and kale are standard salad crops, but lesser known and more exotic greens can add new flavours to meals. Like lettuce, these leafy plants prefer cooler weather. Their tolerance for cold makes them ideal for season extension in the northern garden, where they can be planted earlier and overwinter with protection. This also means that when temperatures rise and when they are exposed to direct sunlight they may tend to bolt (go to seed), but creating shade helps prevent this.

Salads shine when they include a mix of textures, colours, and flavours. We plant a variety of salad greens side by side in the same bed for easier multiple harvests.

Lettuce. We love the many forms, shapes, and textures of lettuce. Red lettuce, oak-leafed varieties, and romaine are among the types we grow. Our favourites include Black Seeded Simpson (a cold-tolerant, pleasantly crunchy heirloom romaine), Royal Oak Leaf, Red Sails, and Red Salad Bowl, as well as other types that are well adapted to colder weather, including Winter Marvel, Annapolis, and Yucalpa.

Paris Island Cos is our standby romaine, while Edox butterhead has been recognized in Vesey's catalogue as a top pick for its crispness and subtle flavour. These lettuce varieties can survive a few degrees of sub-zero temperatures and recover crispness after a light frost has made their leaves go limp. Simple protective structures like cold frames, cloches, tunnels, and lids over raised beds provide additional months of harvestable greens, even through winter, if seeds are planted in late fall.

You can diversify lettuce harvests by planting mesclun, supplied in packages of mixed seed that allow you to plant a whole salad's worth of variation in one seeding. Many seed houses offer mesclun mixes, ranging from mild lettuce blends to a blend of various strongly flavoured greens, including mustard, kale, and arugula.

Spinach. For a slightly more robust salad ingredient than lettuce, plant spinach, starting early in the spring. Spinach will bolt in warm weather; protection from direct sun, regular watering, and succession planting can help maintain your crop. The small round seeds are easy to space out as you plant them. Plant spinach in slightly basic soil; use a layer of mulch to retain moisture and regulate soil temperature.

Arugula. A member of the cabbage and kale family, arugula has a bright, peppery flavour. A low-growing plant with pinnate (feathery) deeply lobed leaves, with four to 10 deep lobes on each side of the leaf, arugula is known scientifically as *Eruca vesicaria*. It grows to a height of 10 centimetres (4 inches) and can be densely planted and harvested as a cutting

Spinach and arugula are easy to grow and add flavour and texture to salads.

DAN RUBIN

green. Seeds are widely available. Some suppliers offer seeds for a perennial variety that can be grown as a continuous crop.

Mustard. Various forms, sizes, and colours of mustard are available. They are excellent cold-tolerant greens to add to a salad mix, from Red Giant to the Asian variant known as mizuna. Interestingly, mizuna was grown experimentally in the International Space Station in 2019.

Kale. Kale is a multi-purpose crop that can be eaten raw in salads, cooked in soups and casseroles, sliced thinly for pasta sauce, or dried in the oven to create kale chips. For salad greens, it is best to plant the tender, flat-leafed varieties such as Red Russian kale, which are hardy survivors that can endure a cold winter.

A sweet and succulent variety from British Columbia's Gulf Islands, our West Coast kale survives the harsh east coast winter, providing a second year of ample green leaves, followed by yellow flowers that form harvestable seed pods. Like other brassicas, kale is a biennial: you get two years of leaf production from each plant if overwintered in the ground.

Nasturtiums. Bob Wildfong, executive director of Seeds of Diversity, notes that nasturtium (now grown as a decorative flower) was listed in the vegetable section of Canadian seed catalogues at the beginning of the 20th century. Nasturtium flowers are spicy, edible, and nutritious and add colour to salads. This easy-to-grow, multi-purpose flowering plant trails down from baskets or grows out over the side of beds, adding garden colour. Add nasturtium flowers and leaves to salads. The young seed pods can be pickled like capers, if harvested when still tender.

Dandelions. Young dandelion greens are a traditional salad crop here in Newfoundland, a common plant that volunteers in lawns and gardens. Rather than seeing dandelions as an invasive weed, remember that the leaves, roots, and flowers have been consumed for centuries. Serve the sweet young leaves with a dressing of oil, lemon juice, and soy sauce or as marinated dandelion greens.

Early starting. We start salad greens from seed in the middle of March. To do this you need a shelf or platform with grow lights (LED or full-spectrum fluorescent tubes) hung above, to provide the illumination that plants need once the seeds sprout. A seed-starting area needs to be warm and have good air circulation. Install a fan to move the air and prevent mould.

Starting seeds in standard-sized pots allows the pots to be packed efficiently into the limited space directly below the lights. Fill pots with sterilized potting mix: this is essential to avoid damping off. Seeds do not need additional nutrients until they sprout; apply a light spray of diluted fertilizer once the sprouts appear above ground.

We place plant pots in large, deep plastic trays filled with water so that the water can soak up into the soil from below. Every three or four days—when the soil is completely dry—we pour water into the bottom of the trays to be wicked up by the soil. If you mist the top of the soil or sprinkle water from a watering can, watering can become a daily chore, but soaking soil from below permits weekly watering until the plants become quite large. When the seedlings are as tall as the pot, pot them on into larger containers.

Hardening off. When greens are about 7 centimetres (3 inches) tall and have been potted on into larger containers, they are ready to move out into the garden. To help them adapt to colder growing

   DAN RUBIN

conditions, harden them off, bringing them out into a cold frame, greenhouse, sunny sheltered location, or a garden bed with a lid. We leave these bedding plants outside when the weather is warm and bring them in each night until conditions are warm enough and they are ready to be planted out.

A cold frame provides young plants with shelter, but be careful: even on a chilly spring day, sunlight entering the cold frame can make it so hot inside that plants may be damaged. Check the temperature inside the box and open the lid if it is above 25°C.

Conditions in our small greenhouse are always moderate, so we move seedlings out to the greenhouse and leave them there at night, instead of bringing them back indoors. We harden them off in this way in early April.

Planting out. Because we plant out into raised beds equipped with protective covers, we set plant seedlings outside earlier than possible in an open, exposed garden. If you plant in rows in a traditional in-ground garden, you can protect plants with floating row cover, a small hoop house, or individual plant covers. We use staggered planting to maximize the space around each plant, rather than planting greens in rows.

When planting out into the garden, disturb roots as little as possible when lifting plants out of the pots. Dig a small hole, just larger than the root ball, line it with bone meal to promote root growth, add compost or fertilizer, lower the plant into the hole, and gently pack soil around the roots. Eliminate any air pockets where the roots could dry out. Water each plant with 0.5 litres (2 cups) of water. Distances between plants vary, depending on their size when mature.

Succession planting. Start seeds at different times so that all seedlings are not ready to plant at the same time. A second seeding indoors makes it easy to create a succession of harvests from garden beds. The goal of succession planting is to create waves of harvestable food by starting the same plant every two weeks in the same bed. Succession planting and intensive growing depend on rich soil with adequate levels of nutrients. This allows you to significantly expand production in a limited space. Seeding directly into the ground, after first planting bedding plants started indoors, also creates succession to extend the harvest.

Fertilizing. Salad greens generally prefer soil with a neutral pH, but brassicas grow better in higher pH soil. Adding dolomite lime, organic fertilizer, compost, and bone meal to the soil boosts plant growth. Adding seaweed or other marine materials before planting helps greens find the nutrients they need for leaf production. If you keep the surroundings cool, with some shade on sunny days, and water daily, you can prevent bolting and generate a continuous harvest. Bolting can be caused by low nitrogen levels and inconsistent moisture as well as higher air temperature or lack of shade.

Weeding. To save work, pack a thick layer of mulch around plants to discourage wild plants from germinating. Mulching makes weeding and thinning easier, because it clarifies which plants need to be pulled out to create growing space for greens. Regular weeding is more manageable than sporadic weeding, because pulling new growth is easier than removing wild plants that have developed deep roots.

Harvesting. A single raised bed can produce more lettuce than a family can eat. A mixed planting is a better use of space: it allows the harvesting of diverse, tasty, and colourful salad greens in a single picking. In addition, many of the plants provide secondary harvests that add variety and flavour; arugula flowers, for example, are excellent in salads; radish seed pods, if harvested while young and crisp, are like a spicy version of snow peas. Harvest salad greens by breaking off or trimming the outer leaves, leaving the inside leaves to continue growing.

Microgreens. Another option for raising salad greens is to

     DAN RUBIN

plant them indoors, harvesting them as microgreens. When they are young, the immature plants have up to four times the nutritional value of mature plants; they are packed with nutrients from the seed plus what they derive from early growth.

Fill trays with 2.5 centimetres (1 inch) of soil as the base medium, then sprinkle on a single type or an assortment of seeds. After the plants sprout and reach about 10 centimetres (4 inches) high, they are ready to harvest. Trim the tops of the plants with a blade or sharp scissors. As the greens continue to grow, putting out new leaves, you can harvest a second, or even a third, time. Once you have finished with the tray, soil and plant remains can be composted.

Microgreens are a valuable and reliable crop. Because they are grown indoors, production sites for microgreens are found across the continent, from the Homestead Garden in Pasadena, California, to the Bonne Bay Cottage Hospital in Norris Point, Newfoundland and Labrador. Microgreens need good airflow to prevent mould, because they grow in tightly packed trays. A fan to move air and a strong lighting source are essential.

17. COOKING GREENS

Leafy greens are also grown to be used as cooked vegetables; they can be steamed, baked, or simmered in soups. Varieties to try include members of the cabbage family, such as mustards and kale. In most cases, plant these as you would salad greens (chapter 16). Since these plants like colder temperatures, they can be started indoors or direct sown into the garden early in the year. Here are some of our favourites.

Asian greens—*bok choy, sui choy, feng qing choi.* Bok choy and its relatives are used in Asian stir-fry dishes, where the mature dark green leaves and white stems provide good crunch and flavour. Feng qing choy (pronounced *feyng cheeng CHOY*) has light green crinkled leaves that look like lettuce, with a slightly piquant cabbage flavour; it is easy to grow in cold conditions, so it is a good choice for overwintering. Other members of the brassica family also do double duty as salad and steamed greens.

Spinach. *Spinacia oleracea* is a well-known member of the Amaranth family and a long-time favourite in European and

American kitchens. Native to western Asia, this leafy green is rich in vitamins A, B, C, E, and K. It does well in colder climates and is easy to grow. Spinach has two forms: smooth-leafed and the crinkled savoy form.

Spinach grows best in moist soil that is rich in nitrogen. It can be sown as soon as the soil warms. The small, smooth, round seeds are easy to plant individually, allowing for good plant spacing. If planted closer than 5 to 7.5 centimetres (2 to 3 inches) apart, spinach can be harvested as it grows, by thinning. Spinach can be started indoors and then planted out, for an earlier crop. Succession planting provides a continuous harvest. Like lettuce, spinach prefers cooler temperatures and bolts if the temperature reaches 30°C or higher. Providing shade and watering on hot days prevents bolting.

Kale. We love kale, raw in salads or as a steamed green. Kale is a biennial brassica that overwinters without protections. We keep cycles of kale going, planting more than once each year, but we also grow kale for seed that we harvest in the second year, when it sets bright yellow blooms and then forms crescent-shaped seed pods. Like other brassicas, kale is vulnerable to cabbage worm: prevent damage by sheltering plants or watering them weekly with salt water.

With so many uses, and because it is so easy to grow, you may want to plant more than one type of kale. If you are saving seeds, different varieties cannot be grown at the same time, as they will cross.

     DAN RUBIN

West Coast kale and other variants of Red Russian kale, dark green, crinkly-leafed Dinosaur kale, and cold hardy Winter Bore are types to try. Kale is also tasty as a sprouted microgreen grown indoors under lights. Kale flowers, whether white or bright yellow, are edible and suitable for adding to salads or as a garnish.

Beets and chard. Beets and chard are members of the same species (*Beta vulgaris*). Direct-seed beet and chard seeds in a staggered pattern, about 10 centimetres (4 inches) apart, to maximize production. Beets form a thick dark red (to yellow) root; chard is the leafy form of the same species. They can be planted in early spring in cooler weather; they sprout quickly and send up dark green leaves with red veins. Chard and beet leaves are high in iron and other nutrients. A continuous harvest of greens for steaming and cooking can be gleaned from the outer leaves.

Beetroot, a reliable, storable root crop, is a staple in Russia, where it is a key ingredient in the sweet-and-sour soup borshch (борщ), usually called *borscht* in North America. Pickled beets are popular, served alongside meat dishes.

By starting beets early indoors or in a cold frame, the harvest can be extended from late February through spring and summer and, with protection, into the depths of the winter. Beets prefer loose soil with a neutral pH and high organic matter. While they like full sun, they do grow with direct sun for part of the day and tolerate some shade, especially in hot summer afternoons. For a late crop, sow again in midsummer, about a month before frost returns.

Reliable varieties include Detroit Dark Red, Cylindra, Early Wonder, and Bull's Blood. A newer variety, Rhonda, is also worth trying; Taunus is recommended for pickling; and some varieties, such as Boldor, are yellow rather than red.

18. BRASSICAS

Members of the cabbage family, collectively known as the brassicas, evolved from a hardy seaside plant (*Brassica oleracea*), now almost extinct. That wild ancestor survives on sea cliffs and in coastal gravel bars where it can withstand salt spray, strong winds, and extreme cold.

These cold-hardy plants known as cabbage, kale, broccoli, broccolini, rapini, cauliflower, Brussels sprouts, and kohlrabi are all cultivars of a single ancestral species. Turnips are from the closely related species *Brassica rapa,* and Oriental cabbages are derived from the Asian subspecies of *Brassica rapa*.

The family tree on page 171 shows how these varied forms have emerged from a single common ancestor through a process of natural variation, along with cultivation and selection by humans over many centuries.

We take advantage of the cold tolerance of these plants, starting them indoors and planting out early in the spring, just as the weather warms up. They are suitable for overwintering under cover or without any additional protection.

Curly kale (bottom) has a coarse texture; Russian kale (like West Coast kale, top) has tender, flatter leaves.

On one visit to British Columbia more than 10 years ago, I returned with seeds for a variety of Russian kale that was growing in the warm, sunny Gulf Islands. This variety of kale not only survives in Newfoundland but can be left in the ground all winter and will come back for a second year of prolific production of leaves before going to seed. This is a good example of winter cold tolerance and demonstrates that many brassicas are biennials. Most (kale, turnip, kohlrabi) flower and produce seed in their second year of growth.

The family tree at the top of the next page shows that humans have created more than one type of food from the same basic plant. We harvest some brassicas when they produce their first leaf bud (cabbage, Brussels sprouts) or as a mature flower (cauliflower, broccoli, broccolini, rapini) formed in the first year of growth, while

     DAN RUBIN

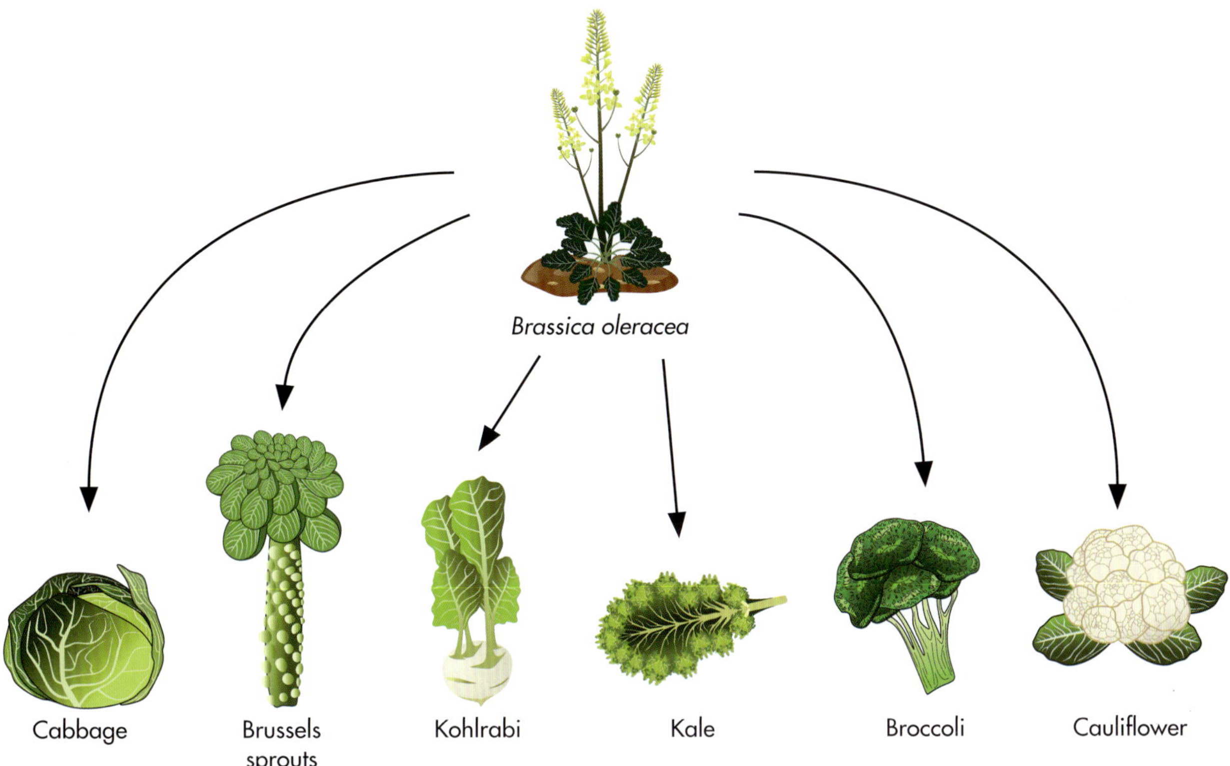

other members of the same family (kale, turnip, kohlrabi) produce a thickened stem or root and wait until the second year to flower and form seed pods.

After harvesting a head of cabbage, you can place the remaining root in damp sand in a cool place (kept just above freezing) and replant it the following year. It will send up a new stalk, flower, and produce seed that can be harvested for replanting the next year.

Growing brassicas. Cabbage family plants prefer soil with a pH between 6 and 7. To create a good soil mix for brassicas, add dolomite lime to make the soil more basic. When we transplant members of the cabbage family into our garden, we put dolomite lime and bone meal in the bottom of the hole before inserting the plant. This gives the soil around the new roots the right pH and encourages root formation.

Spacing plants properly to maximize production requires soil

An entire family of food plants has been developed by humans from a single species in the Brassica family.

with good nutrient levels, so plants can access the necessary nutrients for growth, flowering, and fruiting. To maximize the production of any crop, you need to provide a full range of major and minor nutrients.

We generally plant in a staggered pattern, rather than in rows, to maximize production. Proper spacing is directly relative to the size of the mature plant. In general, because mature cabbage family plants are large, we plant them with 9 inches between plants, measured in each direction. The closer you plant, the more cabbage family plants will shade out competing wild plants.

Cabbage family pests. The main pests of cabbage are slugs and cabbage worms, the caterpillars that emerge from eggs laid by cabbage white butterflies, often mistakenly called cabbage moths. Shallow containers of beer set in the soil entrap and drown slugs. More reliable is the evening slug hunt: visit your garden just before or after dark to remove or kill them.

To prevent cabbage white butterflies from laying eggs, which turn into cabbage worms that consume the tender young leaves, we propose three remedies.

Cover brassicas with a tent of floating row cover to keep the butterflies from the plants. This retains warmth and moisture, while keeping the butterflies from depositing

     DAN RUBIN

eggs. The tent must hold up in wind and should be well sealed to the ground on all sides. The sturdier version of this fabric, sold for large-scale agriculture, is more dependable and lasts longer than the lightweight sheets sold by most stores. Insect mesh is also effective and not as likely as lightweight floating row cover to tear in high winds.

The second remedy is to plant sacrificial plants such as kale or Chinese greens along the edge of the bed, or a companion plant (garlic, calendula, etc.) to discourage butterflies from landing.

A traditional way to eliminate cabbage worm comes from a long-time Pouch Cove resident who grows cabbage in the foundation of an old shed. His huge cabbages caught our eye, growing outdoors without protection. "I go down to the launch," he told us, "and I scoop up a bucket of sea water, bring it back, and I sprinkle it on my plants once a week." Clearly, this method works, thanks to the cabbage family's inherited tolerance for salt. The simplest way to deal with munching caterpillars may be to spray brassicas weekly with sea water or an equivalent.

19. HERBS

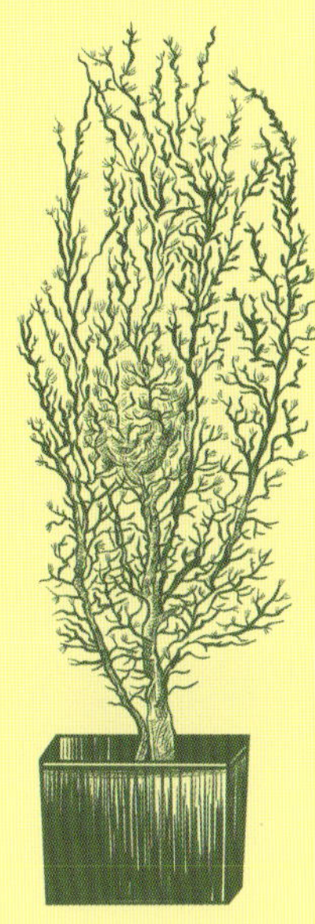

The word *herb* is a non-technical term for any plant grown for its strong flavour or for medicinal purposes. Humans have known about healing herbs for centuries. Many herbs are hardy annuals and perennials that grow well in poor, sandy soil. Common herbs include low shrubs with woody stems as well as more delicate annual plants.

Although some are more cold-tolerant than others, herbs can be grown indoors in containers or overwinter outdoors with some protection. Growing herbs is a good introduction to growing plants for the new gardener. Many are easy to grow. One of the best sources for herb plants and seeds in Canada is Richters, based in Goodwood, Ontario. Their print catalogue lists more than 1,500 seeds and plants.

Here are some of the easiest herbs to grow.

Borage. Borage, with a prolific branching form, is a valuable forage plant for bees. *Borago officinalis*, also called starflower, produces edible deep blue flowers, ideal for salads. The essential oil

has been used medicinally for centuries. It is easy to grow and spreads once established. Borage restores soil fertility by adding nutrients and is a valuable addition to compost. The flavour of the leaves and flowers is reminiscent of that of cucumber and the leaves (both fresh and dried) can be added to soups and stews. In addition to attracting pollinators, borage also repels pests.

Chamomile. Chamomile, a compact member of the daisy family (Asteracea), is grown for its beneficial properties, including calming, sleep support, improved digestion, and blood sugar control. Chamomile flowers smell distinctively sweet. Chamomile is grown mainly for its flowers, which are dried to make a soporific tea. The flowers are easy to harvest. A form of wild chamomile, commonly known as pineappleweed, grows in disturbed areas and along roadsides each summer and fall. The cultivated varieties of chamomile are native to northern Europe,

   DAN RUBIN

where the plant still grows wild. Chamomile is a perennial; it will reseed if its flowers mature and remain on the plant.

Chives. Chives (*Allium schoenoprasum*) are compact bunching onions that grow in clumps, constantly budding off new plants at the edges. One plant in rich soil will become a dense clump within a few years. Chives are easy to grow, invasive, and a true perennial that overwinters nicely with little or no protection. Start chives from seed or ask a friend for a piece of their clump. Chives produce papery purple flowers each summer, but the thin leaves are the main harvest, added to soups, salads, and other dishes. Chives are a great starter plant for novice gardeners. A related species (*Allium tuberosum*), known as garlic chives, is spicier (and less hardy) than regular chives.

Cilantro. Cilantro produces the herb coriander, as its dried seed. Cilantro grows all over the world and is easy to propagate. The best approach in northern climates is to grow cilantro as an annual, reseeding it yearly. Once seeds germinate, cilantro grows well in a sunny, well-drained spot. The plants, part of the Apiaceae family, produce flowers that form in clusters on umbels, and are part of the family that also includes parsley, carrots, cumin, dill, anise, lovage, chervil, and Queen Anne's lace.

Cilantro leaves are used in Mexican cooking. Coriander seeds are harvested, dried, and stored and add a pungent flavour to a variety of dishes. Dried mature seeds can also be used to plant the next year.

Dill. Dill plants grow up to 1 metre (3 feet) tall in rich soil with full sun and must be planted yearly. Its flowers form in umbels, clustered on a common stem. Dill, generally grown for its seeds, which form after the flowers have been pollinated, is commonly used to flavour pickles. The feathery leaves are also used in soups and stews.

Mint. Members of the mint family (Lamiaceae), distinguished by square stems and strong scent, are often used in cooking and for tea. A wide range of mint is easy to grow. Because mint becomes invasive, it is best grown in containers. Mint leaves are easy to harvest and dry. Plants can be grown from seed but are also easy to transplant, as they are vigorous and root quickly.

Oregano. Grown as a perennial, oregano pairs well with tomato-based sauces and is used extensively in Italian cooking. A member of the mint family, oregano is native to Eurasia and has been grown there for centuries, since being brought into the garden from the wild. Dried oregano leaves are more fragrant than fresh leaves and may be stored in a cool dry place for several years before losing their potency. Consider growing fresh oregano in a pot on a sunny windowsill or just outside the back door. Oregano overwinters and spreads unless contained. Its leaves and white or pink blossoms are used in cooking. The forms of oregano and marjoram that survive in northern climates are called flowering oregano, a harsher tasting relative of those varieties that grow in warmer locations.

Parsley. Grown as a salad green or as an herb to be dried and

DAN RUBIN

stored, parsley is a biennial. It originally came from the shores of the Mediterranean but is now grown worldwide. A range of parsley subtypes is available, from the more strongly flavoured Italian varieties to flat-leafed types. If parsley is planted in a container, it can be harvested for two years before going to seed.

Sage. Grey fuzzy sage leaves provide a visual accent nestled among garden greens. Some varieties have variegated (yellow and green) leaves; dark-green-leaved varieties are also available. Sage will grow as a perennial if protected with a layer of mulch or row cover over winter. Dried leaves are easy to harvest, either by cutting branches when green and hanging them to dry indoors, or by stripping them in the fall when the plant is dormant and leaves have dried on the plant.

Sage (above) and oregano (below) can be harvested before or after flowering. Leaves and flowers can be dried and used in recipes.

Sage is a secret ingredient in Italian tomato sauces, adding a piquant, slightly bitter taste. It produces attractive clusters of blue or white flowers when it blooms.

Savory. Summer savory (*Satoreja hortensis*) is a favourite herb in Newfoundland and Labrador. An annual with a 2,000-year history of culinary use, it originated on the shores of the Mediterranean and is closely related to winter savory, also known as mountain savory, a form that grows as a perennial. Savory likes light, loamy soil and moderate watering and prefers to grow in full sun. Dried savory adds a warm, musky flavour to poultry stuffing and other dishes. Seeds can be planted directly into the garden in late April or started in pots indoors and planted out. Savory is ideal for container growing. Both summer and winter savory branches, if pinched at the top of the growing stems, create even more harvestable leaves. To dry the leaves, break off the stems at the base, bundle, and hang indoors in a cool, dry place.

Thyme. Thyme is a low-growing herb. The variant "creeping thyme" can be planted as a ground cover, releasing a pleasant odour when crushed underfoot. The hardy thyme plant grows perennially once established. Harvesting is easy: trim off growing tips with

DAN RUBIN

scissors or pinch off with your fingers. Thyme is used in traditional recipes across Europe. Among the 26 types available in the Richters catalogue are varieties that have lemon or orange flavour. These are grown for their fragrance; not all are pleasant for use in cooking.

These 11 herbs are recommended for ease of cultivation and as an introduction to the world of medicinal plants. Whether planted from seed or transplanted as bedding plants purchased from a nursery, herbs generally do not need rich soil, but they do like well-drained locations, in the garden or in containers. Herbs in containers can be brought indoors during the winter to grow on a sunny windowsill, where they are handy for incorporation in a wide range of dishes and food traditions.

Basil. Basil is not included in the list of easy-to-grow herbs because it needs consistent warmth and protection from wind to do well. But it thrives indoors and, during the warm months, sheltered in a greenhouse. Fresh basil can be kept alive through the winter on a sunny windowsill. We harvest and dry basil leaves to use in cooking. There are more than 100 varieties of basil, including Genovese, lemon, Thai, and Persian. A popular way to preserve basil is to make

pesto, a thick sauce blended from basil, pine (or other) nuts, olive oil, and salt. Pesto can be stored in jars or frozen in pouches.

Harvesting herbs. Herbs are ideal for drying after being harvested. The technique is simple: pull the whole plant, break off or cut branches and flower stems, and hang to dry in a warm, well-ventilated space. Do not dry herbs in an oven, dehydrator, or other heated space as the heat evaporates the volatile oils that are the reason you have harvested them. Every fall, branches of oregano, thyme, rosemary, and sage tied in bundles hang from hooks in our kitchen where they dry over a few days in the warm air.

Harvest herbs during the day when the leaves are dry. Spread large branches or leaves on a window screen or in a basket indoors in a cool location, with good air circulation, where moving air will gradually remove the moisture from the foliage. Harvesting after the plants flower is also possible. Although young leaves produce a more subtle flavour, the more robust flavour of the flowers is also

     DAN RUBIN

appealing. If you pay attention to their size as the leaves expand and the plant flowers, you can determine when to harvest.

Once fully dry (twigs should snap, not bend), remove the dried leaves from the stem, stripping them by hand. Store the dried leaves, whole or crumbled, in bottles or zipper-sealed bags for later use. Sealed containers help maintain their potency, but in a year or two they should be replaced with fresher herbs. Extend the shelf life of dried herbs by freezing them after drying.

Healing herbs. Many herbs have a long history as medicinal plants; this is part of a long-established tradition of natural medicine. Herbs are important in traditional Chinese medicine and extensive knowledge of them is also held by Indigenous healers around the world. Many research sources provide information about healing herbs. Those who carry Indigenous and traditional knowledge are restoring appreciation for these plants and their medicinal uses as herbal teas, tinctures, and salves.

20. CUCURBITS

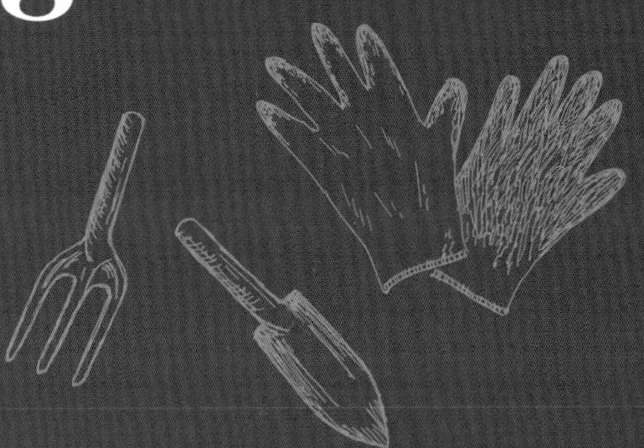

The Cucurbitae (Cucurbit or Gourd family) is a large group of interrelated species that includes cucumbers, pumpkins, squash, citron, melons, and hundreds of wild species. These vining plants produce a large fleshy body, technically a berry. The Cucurbitae include 975 species of plants native to temperate and tropical areas. Most are sensitive to temperatures near the freezing point, which limits their geographic distribution. Cucurbits are fast-growing prostrate (spreading) plants and climbing vines. Their long-stalked palmate leaves alternate along the stem. Many cucurbits send out tendrils that curl around upright structures to find purchase and support the stem.

Individual plants generally have both male or female flowers, so pollination depends on pollen transportation from a male to a female flower. This fact is the key to isolating cucurbit varieties to keep them from crossing. Not all cucurbits can cross, but tales of *squmpkins*, *gourdchinis*, and *cucamelons* or *cuculoupes* show that this can happen, if related plants are grown too near each other or if bees carry pollen between plants.

GROUP A — *CUCURBITA PEPO*	
Summer squash	yellow crookneck, straight neck, zucchini, scallop, pattypan squash
Winter squash	acorn and spaghetti squash varieties
Gourds	many ornamental non-edible types
Pumpkins	Cinderella, Big Tom, Jack o'Lantern, Small Sugar, Sugar Pie, Jackpot, others
GROUP B — *CUCURBITA MOSCHATA*	
Winter squash	butternut squash
Pumpkins	Cheese, Dickinson Field, Golden Cushaw, Kentucky Field
GROUP C — *CUCURBITA MAXIMA*	
Winter squash	Hubbard varieties
Pumpkins	Big Max, King of the Mammoths, Mammoth Chile, Atlantic Giant
Ornamental squash	Aladdin, Turk's Turban
GROUP D — *CUCURBITA MIXTA*	
Pumpkins	Cushaw, Japanese Pie, Tennessee "Sweet Potato," Mixta Gold
GROUP E — *CUCUMIS SATIVUS*	
Cucumbers	common slicing and pickling cucumber, except the Armenian type
	Beit Alpha cucumber
	Lemon cucumber
GROUP F — *CUCUMIS MELO*	
Cucumber	Armenian "snake cucumber," also known as Serpent Melon
Melons	all muskmelons, including cantaloupe, casaba, honeydew
GROUP G — *CITRULLUS LANATUS*	
Watermelons	
Citrons	

Cucurbit flowers have five white or yellow petals. When pollinated, they produce a pepo, a fleshy, many-seeded enlarged berry with a tough rind, that protects the seeds and provides food for them once they germinate. The large fleshy fruit also protects seeds from lower temperatures. Seeds are elliptical and flattened, and some have wings for seed dispersal.

Seven separate species of cucurbits are listed at left. Within each species group, plants can cross-pollinate, but they usually not do this across species boundaries.

If two different species of squash, pumpkin, or cucumber are grown side by side, they are unlikely to cross, because they belong to different species. To keep two plants in the same species from crossing, grow them more than 30 metres (100 feet) apart.

By hand-pollinating, some gardeners eliminate the possibility of cucurbits crossing: they pluck a male flower and use it to dust female flowers on the same or nearby plants of the same species. The shorter female flowers, identified by a bulge at the base, generally form later than the male flowers. To ensure that no crossing occurs after hand-pollinating, tie a paper bag around the female flower until it wilts and the fruit begins to expand. Once the fruit begins to form, remove the bag, or let it rot away, and the result will be true breeding.

Pumpkins, squash, cucumbers, and their

relatives are known for ease of growing and for the quantity and storability of the food they produce. When you grow pumpkins or squash, the sweet meat from these large fruits can be cured in the sun then stored in a cool dry place (kept above freezing) to be turned into delicious steamed vegetables, soups, and pie fillings.

With pumpkins to be found in four of the seven cucurbit species, it helps to know which varieties you are growing, if you want to save seed for future replanting.

Some practical tips. Because many of these plants originated in the tropics of Central America, they do like warmth. It is usually best to grow cucumbers in a greenhouse, although they can be grown outdoors with protection from wind and cold. Squash and pumpkins grow best in mounds or raised beds. Because they are heavy feeders, planting them directly in a mound of compost or manure is one way to ensure a bountiful harvest.

As the vines spread out across the ground, train them by moving them out from underfoot on paths and in grass. Trellising takes advantage of vertical space. Using whatever narrow strips of wood are at hand, build a trellis or grating, either vertical or leaning against a support or wall, onto which the vines can spread and grow. This supports the heavy pumpkins and squashes when they form, keeping them off the ground, away from mould and slugs and other creatures.

Cucamelons (*Melothira scabra*) are a miniature cucurbit, native to Central America. They are a recent hit in local gardens.

As with other garden crops, soil quality is critical. Rich, sandy, well-drained soil in a sunny location, sheltered from wind, is ideal for growing cucurbits. As they grow, they can be fed periodically with fresh compost or dissolved fertilizers. The massive Atlantic Giant pumpkins (some weighing more than 450 kilograms [1,000 pounds] are fed soured milk, which shows that additional calcium as well as nitrogen will enhance fruit production.

Growing large, tasty squash and pumpkins depends on direct sun and warmth, sturdy support, and generous applications of organic matter. The large fleshy fruits consume considerable water, so a weekly soaking and feeding is advised, unless a heavy rainfall has occurred.

Starting seeds indoors provides a sheltered, heated space for early growth. After sprouting, the vine grows quickly and the roots need

DAN RUBIN

room to grow, so pot seedlings on into a larger container before moving them into the garden. If danger of frost persists after they have been planted, cover them with a cloche or floating row cover, or plant under a high tunnel. The covers or cloche can be left in place as the weather warms, until the plants need more room to send out vines and set flowers. Make sure that they have adequate ventilation on sunny days, so that they do not get too hot.

Cucurbits need to be protected from strong winds that can damage or even uproot them. Installing lattice fencing on the windward side breaks the force of the wind, while still allowing fresh air to flow through.

Harvesting cucurbits is a time for celebration. Squash and pumpkin can be hollowed out, filled with various ingredients, and roasted or steamed, or pureed and made into spicy or creamy soups. Whether baked in pies at Thanksgiving, carved into Halloween decorations, or stored for later use as a steamed or roasted vegetable, the yellow-orange flesh is sweet in flavour and high in nutrients.

Storage, however, is a challenge. Harvest squash and pumpkins after the stem has changed from green to brown. To harvest, cut through the stem, rather than breaking it, to avoid leaving a scar which can invite rot. After they are removed from the vine, the large fruits should be cured outdoors in a warm place, in full sun. Once the skin has dried and hardened, they are ready for storage. Unless you have a cool, dry storage space that never freezes, it is best to store them indoors in a location with good air circulation, such as a warm, dry basement. Because squash and pumpkin retain water, they are vulnerable to spoilage.

Cucumbers. Growing cucumbers requires protection from wind and cold, so they are best cultivated in a greenhouse or some other form of shelter. Start seeds indoors under lights—we sow one seed per cell or 10-centimetre (4-inch) pot in mid-April—then transplant them into larger containers in May, and plant them out into the greenhouse as soon as there is warmth in the soil.

Growing in containers, or in the ground, the vines climb, so they require strings or a trellis for support. Whether you have planted pickling cucumbers (the smaller, bumpy variation), standard cucumbers, or the Long English varieties, they need rich soil with lots of organic material and consistent watering to produce a good harvest. Feeding weekly with diluted fish fertilizer, compost tea, or seaweed booster improves production.

Cucumbers can be left on the vine until needed. Harvest when still young and tender, before the fruits turn yellow (they are fruits, even though we use them as a vegetable). Once harvested, store cucumbers in a cool, humid place, such as the refrigerator vegetable drawer. They can also be hung in a basket or placed in a root cellar; but check weekly for spoilage. You can preserve cucumbers by turning them into dill pickles, sweet pickles, or spicy pickles and

relish. Look online for recipes for quick refrigerator pickles made with vinegar, salt, and spices, as well as the traditional pickles that are slow-fermented in brine.

Summer squash. Certain varieties of squash, known generically as summer squash, are grown for immediate use. These include zucchini, crookneck, straight neck, and scalloped forms, among others.

Our standard advice when people ask how to grow zucchini: "throw the seeds and run." These plants can be so prolific that just one plant can overwhelm you with squash that quickly grow so large that they are more suitable for baking than frying.

Like the other cucurbits, we start seeds indoors and transplant out into the garden after potting on to make sure our plants have plenty of room for their roots. These plants are hardier than cucumbers, so they can go out into the garden with or without protection, although they do best in a sunny spot without too much wind shear.

For best production, make sure summer squash plants have room to spread out and top-dress with manure or compost. Planting into a

mound of compost is a favourite way to grow any squash or pumpkin.

Zucchini and crookneck squash, sliced thin then sauteed gently in olive oil, sea salt, and a splash of balsamic vinegar, until just tender, is an enduring favourite in our home.

Winter squash. The winter squash varieties, so called because they develop a harder skin and can be stored through the winter, have flesh that can be described as sweet or buttery, depending on the variety you grow. The most common winter squash varieties include acorn, delicata, spaghetti, and butternut as well as the true winter squashes, members of the *Cucurbitae maxima* species, that include banana, buttercup, and sweet mama types. The University of Illinois website lists 37 types of winter squash. But not all of these can be grown in colder locations.

Recommended for northern gardeners are Sweet Reba acorn squash, Honeynut butternut, open pollinated Delicata, green Hokkaido, and the standard spaghetti varieties. Baby Blue Hubbard is a favourite for consistent production and sweet taste. By consulting seed catalogues and paying attention to length of growing season, the search for the best, most productive winter squash can become an enjoyable annual activity.

If the seeds that you order are OP (open pollinated, true breeding) you can save and replant them, but F1 (hybrid) plants produce seeds that may diverge from type. Although many valuable hybrid seeds have been developed, the growing appreciation for home seed saving has added a stream of heritage varieties to what is now available.

After harvesting winter squash in the fall, cure them by leaving them in the sun for several warm days. This allows the skin to dry out and harden. Storing at room temperatures in dry surroundings is the key to keeping squash for months.

Pumpkins. Pumpkins are a form of winter squash with a round shape and yellow to orange skin. Well known for their association with Halloween, our North American version of the Day of the Dead, pumpkins are often carved into jack-o'-lanterns. Interestingly, the first fruits carved in this way were actually turnips, not pumpkins.

Unless you are setting out to try grow the Atlantic Giants that can weigh in at more than 450 kilograms (1,000 pounds), pumpkins will grow well if planted directly into soil in a mound or bed rich in organic matter. The giant varieties require regular feeding. Pumpkins can be started indoors under lights, like other winter squash and transplanted into the garden once the weather has warmed. Most varieties are tough enough to endure a touch of frost. Their vines spread out as they grow. Once the fruit forms, provide some insulation from the ground to prevent mould and protect the fruit from slugs and snails with a board or trellis.

Pumpkins can range in size from the diminutive Jack Be Little to the Atlantic Giants. Their flesh and seeds are an excellent form of storable food; if cured after harvest they can then be stored for sure through the winter. We recommend the following OP varieties to northern gardeners: Long Pie, Howden, Casper (white skin), and Long Island Cheese, a renowned heirloom. Pepitas are grown particularly for roasted seed.

All of these varieties need about 100 days of growth to maturity. Starting seeds indoors and planting out early are recommended to provide for a good fall harvest.

Melons. Melons, like squash, grow on vines that will climb up a trellis or spread across the ground. Because they require added protection and warmth, they may not be suitable for outdoor cultivation unless you have protection from wind and cold, which can be achieved by adding row cover or planting in a sheltered spot. We grow melons inside our greenhouse, where the additional warmth provides an excellent place for them to spread out, flower, and produce fruit. Both watermelons and the various musk melons (cantaloupe, honeydew, casaba, Persian) do well in rich soil with consistent watering and feeding.

Halona is our favourite cantaloupe, while Pixie produces smaller fruit, making it ideal for a shorter growing season. Almost all the melon seeds available are F1 hybrids; two heirloom, OP varieties to consider are Rocky Ford and Hale's Best, both available from High Mowing Seeds in Vermont. Many hybrid melons were developed to create resistance to mildew, a form of mould commonly found in the warm, damp conditions favoured by these warmth-loving plants.

Directions for planting melons are essentially the same as for other cucurbits: starting under lights in early spring, followed by potting on to larger containers before planting in the greenhouse or a protected outdoor space. Although we have not grown watermelons

DAN RUBIN

ourselves, others on the east coast of Canada have had luck with these summer favourites.

Gourds. These squash are grown to be dried and used for decoration; in traditional cultures, they also provided containers for transporting, saving, or serving liquids. Grown in much the same way as melons or squash, they are harvested after their skins harden, and are then cured and dried. They need a warm, protected space to do well. For details of how to grow and use these fruits, visit the Canadian Gourd Society website.

21. NIGHTSHADES

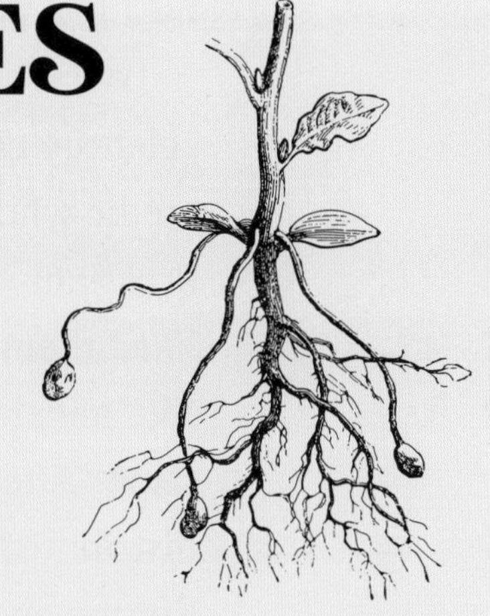

The nightshade family (Solanaceae) includes three important edible plants: tomatoes, potatoes, and peppers, as well as some poisonous species, including the deadly nightshade. Understanding how this family has made its way into our gardens reminds us that each of these plants contains toxic compounds in its leaves and stem.

Tomatoes, peppers, and potatoes were carried across the Atlantic from the Americas as part of the Columbian Exchange. While maize (corn) was rapidly adopted by Europeans because it was similar to other grains already under cultivation, other plants took much longer to be recognized as food. Turkeys, similar to the wild birds already hunted for food, were rapidly adopted as farm livestock. But members of the Solanaceae family were considered botanical oddities and shunned by cooks for centuries. Eggplants were described by John Gerard in his 1633 herbal as "venomous and deadly," while tomatoes were called "love apples" and considered poisonous.

Potatoes similarly languished in obscurity for centuries because they were considered toxic and later because of their bland flavour.

Even though a recipe for potatoes fried with onions made it into the famous *Larousse Gastronomique* in the 1700s, few considered potatoes edible. One regional European parliament even declared the potato responsible for leprosy. But they were still being grown by a few poorer farmers as a reliable source of food.

What the potato needed, to get it firmly onto the menu, was a celebrity chef. Along came Antoine-Augustine Parmentier, a French medic who was forced to eat potatoes after he was captured by the Prussians during the Seven Years War. He actually found that he liked them, so later, as a pharmacist and then adviser to King Louis XVI and Marie Antoinette, he launched the potato into culinary fame. After recruiting the king as a fan of the plant, Parmentier distributed seed potatoes to French farmers, and they spread across Europe and into Britain from there.

The cultivation of potatoes became a standard part of food production across Europe until potato blight created the Irish Potato Famine in the 1800s. The blight ravaged crops across northern Europe, forcing waves of migrants to emigrate to North America. But for more than a century before that, potatoes were reliable food, easy to grow and store. This "bread of the poor" was celebrated by the emperor Napoleon Bonaparte, whose armies relied on them for portable food supplies as they rolled through country after country. Potatoes became a primary source of food security for Germany and Russia in the 1700s and were widely recognized as the fuel of war.

It took even longer for tomatoes to make their way into the cooking of Italy and other cultures around the shores of the Mediterranean. According to food historian Silvano Serventi, the meeting of tomatoes and pasta was "inevitable," but it was not until the 1800s that their important role in sauces and soups was confirmed.

Tomato recipes only appeared in regional Italian cookbooks toward the end of the 19th century. In 1891, a resident of Florence,

   DAN RUBIN

Pellegrino Artusi, wrote the first truly pan-Italian cookbook, including recipes for *salsa di pomodoro*. Tomato sauce has since become a familiar staple, an essential for classic Italian-American cooking.

Pizza, invented in Naples as street food, was originally made with a range of toppings, from oil to anchovies. Pizza topped with tomato sauce was one variation, until Pizza Margherita, named for the wife of the king of the Two Sicilies, was announced as her favourite and became the best-known version, topped with tomato, slices of mozzarella cheese, and torn basil leaves.

To round out the history of the origins of the Solanaceae, consider the eggplant, a nightshade that produces round or long fruit with shiny black-purple, striped, or mottled skin. The eggplant entered Middle Eastern cuisine after travelling from China and India, where it had been cultivated for thousands of years. The Moors brought eggplant into Spain and eastern Europe, and it became popular there. It was carried across the Atlantic to the Americas in the 1500s but did not catch on in the New World at first.

Nightshades need a source of magnesium and good drainage. Tomatoes, peppers, and eggplants prefer warm surroundings, because the plants originated in semi-tropical locations. Although we plant potatoes outdoors in garden rows or raised beds, we grow tomatoes, peppers, and eggplants in more sheltered spaces inside a greenhouse or in the tented structure we call our tomato house.

The tomato house is a sturdy, peaked-roof, wood-framed structure built from recycled wood, with ends sealed with plastic, and a roll of plastic stapled down on the windward side then rolled over the top and held down on the other side by the weight of two pieces of 2-by-3 lumber, screwed together along the downwind edge of the plastic sheeting. This allows us to open the structure when the sun is shining, vent heat, rolling off the plastic covering on sunny days and during the warmest months of the year.

Our spring routine starts with planting pepper, tomato, and eggplant seeds indoors in early April in plant pots or trays filled with sterilized potting soil, sprouting them under lights, then transplanting them into individual pots later in April, and planting

     DAN RUBIN

them out into the garden in early May inside protective structures.

Potatoes. Images sent by friends living in Ecuador, where potatoes were originally grown high in the Andes and in river valleys flowing down to the Pacific, show outdoor markets with hundreds of varieties of potato tubers for sale, in a huge range of shapes and colours.

In Newfoundland and Labrador, researcher Ken Proudfoot spent years creating new potato varieties by crossing heirloom strains that he found growing in outport communities along the shores of our island. Each variety has its particular uses and preferred growing conditions. The result: dozens of new locally adapted potato strains.

Proudfoot's brilliant work produced potatoes prized by local growers that are no longer available commercially as potato seed. These include red-, white-, and blue-skinned tubers that are exceptionally resistant to potato canker. Although some local gardeners still grow these valuable heritage varieties, it is difficult to source the seed for these types that are so well adapted to local growing conditions.

Common scab, a fungal disease that affects potatoes if they are grown in high pH soils, can be counteracted to a certain extent by adding peat to the soil to lower the pH. Where potatoes are grown in a bed or garden row, do not lime the soil because that raises the pH and encourages scab to form on the tuber's surface.

Because potatoes need a trace amount of magnesium to do well, it is included in commercial potato fertilizers. In a small bed or garden row, you can supplement soil magnesium by scattering 125 millilitres (0.5 cup) of Epsom salts (magnesium sulfate) per 2 square metres (20 square feet) or by adding 5 millilitres (1 teaspoon) of the white powder to each litre (4 cups) of water you use. Potatoes also need a good supply of nitrogen and potassium for plant growth and phosphorus for fruiting, flowering, and root growth.

Potatoes are traditionally planted in rows or drills, hilled up with more soil as they grow, to promote tuber formation and protect them from sunlight, which causes them to turn green. The presence of the green pigment chlorophyll signals the buildup of a bitter, toxic substance, solanine. To prevent greening, cover the tubers with soil and mulch, as they grow.

Potatoes can also be grown in raised beds. Whether planting in rows or beds, proper spacing of plants is important to maximize production. We plant seed potatoes (small potatoes from the previous year's crop or a cut section of a larger potato, sliced and allowed to air-dry before planting) about 30 centimetres (1 foot) apart. Each potato's "eyes" sprout to produce a new plant.

This is an example of *vegetative reproduction*, since each year's crop grows from the previous year's tubers, without going through fertilization of flowers and seed formation between generations. Potato plants do flower and produce seed above ground, but growers

generally rely on planting seed potatoes for annual production. This way, there is no chance of two varieties crossing; and the strains that grow well in particular soils or locations can be kept true for centuries.

Potatoes like full sun, slightly acidic soil, and plenty of organic matter, but it is best to avoid fresh manure. In our region, people traditionally used caplin (a silvery fish that spawns on beaches each year) to feed their potatoes; fish waste can boost soil fertility, either in raw form, dug in before the fall planting, or added in the spring in the form of fish compost. Seaweed is another highly desirable, traditional soil amendment that provides micronutrients that potatoes need, including the essential magnesium. With rich soil, warm sun, and adequate water, about 10 times the weight of the potatoes that you plant as seed can be harvested.

For successful potato cultivation, hill soil over the potatoes as they grow; after planting, do not water until sprouts appear above ground to keep the seed from rotting. Keep soil moist but not wet, watering only if there is a period without a soaking rain. Once the plants produce white or purple blooms, you can harvest the small, new potatoes that form along the underground stems.

Commercial seed potatoes are standard varieties that may not be well suited to your location. Choose the right variety for your region and climate. If an established gardener or farmer near you maintains a unique variety, ask for a few seed potatoes; your neighbours may have small potatoes suitable for seed that they are willing to share.

Potatoes can also be grown in bins, boxes, barrels, and buckets. The double challenge with any form of container growing is to provide rich, well-drained soil and sufficient drainage to allow excess moisture to drain out. Growing in a restricted space means that only two or three potato plants can be planted in each 20-litre (5-gallon) bucket. Growing in rows or beds is more efficient than container growing for potatoes, unless garden space is restricted.

Planting in the ground allows nature to provide natural ecological support to resist pests and build soil fertility from year to year.

Another innovative approach to container potato gardening is the "potato tower," a crib or box of wooden slats, or a square frame of shipping pallets, into which potatoes are planted, in layers, with each planting covered successively with soil, straw, mulch, or compost. The potatoes sprout and continue to grow toward the light, ideally filling the crib with a crop of tubers to be harvested at the end of the season. Some gardeners have had success with this; others wonder if it is any more efficient to plant potatoes vertically than in the ground.

Potatoes take up more space than many other crops and may not be the most effective use of garden space. But if you have a field in which rows of these plants can grow, and a cool, dry storage space for winter, it is satisfying to produce, store, and cook your own tubers, without chemical fertilizers and poisons.

Potatoes are susceptible to a range of diseases, including canker and scab, as well as Colorado potato beetle, blight, blackleg (a bacterial disease), and rot caused by fungal spores or bacteria. Rather than providing a prescription for each disease, remember that good drainage, careful variety selection, and maintaining low pH soil ensures plant health and prevents diseases and pests. Rotating grow location yearly helps replenish the soil and avoid the buildup of disease organisms.

If you see evidence of disease, such as discoloration or wilting of the stems or leaves of potato plants, remove and discard these parts to keep the plants healthy. When possible, use potato seed that is certified as canker- and scab-free. In some cases, traditional varieties available from friends and neighbours may resist scab even better than the certified varieties.

Wait until the leaves are yellow before harvesting mature potatoes, digging them up carefully with a cultivator or fork, while trying not

     DAN RUBIN

to pierce or bruise the tubers. After laying them out in the sun for a day to dry and cure, they can be stored in buckets or woven bags and moved to a root cellar or other cool, dry area for long-term storage.

To keep stored potatoes from sprouting, protect them from moisture and light. But, as spring approaches, stored potatoes begin to send out runners, long thin sprouts, in anticipation of the new growing year. This actually helps prepare seed potatoes for planting. Another storage option is to leave them in the ground over the winter; potatoes generally survive and will sprout and produce a crop the next year.

Tomatoes. We start more than a dozen varieties of heirloom tomatoes from seed, searching for types that grow well in a cold climate and produce ripe fruit in our short summer growing season. We avoid the standard beefsteak, sweet million, and plum tomatoes sold by nurseries. Many others are better adapted to our climate.

Here are some tomato varieties that we recommend to northern gardeners:

- *Alma*: heirloom variety, available from Goddess Grown Heirlooms
- *Azoychka*: yellow beefsteak, originally from Eastern Europe
- *Bellstar*: reliable cold-tolerant type, available from High Mowing Seeds
- *Bonnie's Best*: medium, smooth-skinned, round, reliable producer
- *Carbon*: grown in New England, a well-known heritage variety
- *Casady's Folly*: paste tomato variety, available from Greta's Organic
- *Chalk's Early Jewel*: renowned discovery of James Chalk, in Pennsylvania, 1899
- *Cherokee Purple*: widely available heirloom with striking deep red/purple colour
- *Galena's Yellow*: prolific producer of extra-sweet yellow cherry tomatoes
- *Moskvich*: Russian heirloom, available from High Mowing Seeds
- *Paul Robeson*: an early tomato with dark purple to black skin
- *Roadstar*: hybrid recommended by Ross Traverse as a prolific producer
- *Red Alert*: reliable medium greenhouse tomato
- *Roma*: grown for tomato paste and sauce, available from multiple sources
- *Sasha's Altai*: short-season, cold-tolerant variety, available from Urban Harvest

‮• *Scotia*: well-known, reliable, cold-tolerant variety, widely available

‮• *San Marzano*: the "tomato that ate California," ideal for canning, originally from Sicily

‮• *SubArctic Maxi*: widely available cold-tolerant commercial variety

‮• *Vantage*: heritage tomato in our region, grown outdoors or in greenhouse

‮• *Zapotec*: ribbed, long-season beefsteak

If you look beyond the usual commercial suppliers for seed, you will find even more tomato varieties. And if you join the Canadian heritage seed organization Seeds of Diversity, membership will give you access to a members' catalogue that lists more than 1,000 varieties of tomato seed, to be ordered from fellow gardeners and growers. Membership is free. Entire pages devoted to red, yellow, pink to purple, and multicoloured tomatoes can be found online and in the annual printed catalogue, offering an entire world of tomato choices! Cold-tolerant species are also available from regional seed houses and local suppliers. Consider trying a few new types each year, as you search for those that grow best and deliver the best flavour.

Tomatoes originally grew as weedy perennials in tropical and subtropical climates on the mountainsides of Central America, where they evolved and were bred by Indigenous growers. Even those cultivars that have adapted to tolerate colder environments grow best in a warm place. You may be lucky to live in a local pocket of warmth. But in most northern gardens, shelter is needed to protect tomato plants; we rely on protective structures to keep out wind and create insulation from the cold. With these structures, we add up to two months to the growing season.

Our home seed collection includes more than 35 types of tomatoes

DAN RUBIN

we have collected from seed suppliers and fellow growers. In early spring (late March to mid-April), we plant one seed in each corner of a 10-centimetre (4-inch) plastic pot, filled with sterilized potting soil. The pots are placed on a table in a warm basement space under grow lights set to 16 hours on, eight hours off, to provide light and warmth. Once the plants sprout (in about four to seven days), we place the lights as close to them as possible. We place plant pots in large plastic trays and water them by filling the trays with 2.5 centimetres (1 inch) of water every four to eight days, to provide a steady supply until the soil dries out.

Once the plants are about 10 centimetres (4 inches high), they are potted on into individual 10- to 15-centimetre (4- to 6-inch) pots for further growth and root expansion. This usually happens toward the end of April/early May. The transplants continue to grow under lights, reaching 15 centimetres (6 inches) by mid-May, then they move to the greenhouse for hardening off.

By the end of May, sometimes earlier, weather-dependent, we have strong plants with thick stems, ready for planting. Our tomato plants do not go into an open bed but are planted in the soil inside our greenhouse, or in the tomato house, and in a few containers on our deck once they are fully hardened off. These structures protect them from the occasional spring frost, cold winds, and onslaughts of rain and snow.

Mulching is also a key to tomato production. We have tried planting through red plastic mulch, with holes cut in the plastic. We have been told that the reflected red light makes a difference in

fruit production and ripening, but we have not yet confirmed this. Other forms of mulch such as grass clippings, compost, and other materials that feed the soil can make a difference, feeding the soil and suppressing germination of wild plants.

Tomato plants are either determinate (bush type) or indeterminate (vining). The compact bush types, including Early Wonder, Fargo, Golden Girl, Roma, Lady Finger, Lunch Box, Napoli, Northern Delight, Principe Borghese, San Marzano, and Tiny Tim, are particularly suitable for container growing inside a greenhouse or on a sunny deck. Indeterminate vining types require support as they grow upward, set flowers, and then fruit, while continuing to climb.

We use metal tomato cages in our greenhouse to support indeterminate tomato plants. To further extend vertical growth, tie strings to horizontal stringers above the plants and wind the tomato stems around the strings, as they grow, to guide them upward. Another option, for both determinate and indeterminate varieties, is to plant the seeds in soil-filled grow bags that hang overhead in the greenhouse so the plants will hang down below the bag as they grow.

     DAN RUBIN

We feed our tomato plants weekly, watering with weed, compost, and fish teas made by diluting water-composted concentrate, purchased from local suppliers, to increase growth and plant health. Weeding is minimal but we do remove any wild plants that struggle up through the mulch. The weed-and-feed routine continues through the warm months, and we gradually open and then remove the rolled plastic over our tomato house. In the greenhouse, by opening vents and then doors and with a fan installed in front of the upper exhaust vent, we keep temperatures moderate; maintain an ambient temperature below 30°C (86°F).

Once the tomatoes set fruit, remove the suckers (the new branches that appear as tiny sprouts inside the elbow of the branching leaf stems) before they develop their own flowers and fruit. Later, remove all extraneous branches and leaves to concentrate nutrients in the ripening fruit and increase their size and flavour.

Our tomatoes generally do not begin to ripen until late summer or early fall. The tomato harvest begins in late August and continues through the decreasing temperatures of September and into October, when we find ourselves overwhelmed with ripe tomatoes. We preserve tomatoes by canning them, making sauces and salsa, and by pickling green tomatoes using the quick pickle method (bottling them with a mixture of vinegar, salt, sugar, and spices).

Two varieties of tomato, grown for decades here on the east coast of Canada, have proven to be real winners: Vantage, a regional heirloom well suited to greenhouse cultivation, and Red Alert, a vining

tomato that produces prolific mid-sized fruit. We obtained seeds for these varieties from local nursery operator and author Ross Traverse and have been sharing these seeds with other growers to ensure that we keep these varieties of tomato available.

We continue to seek out interesting tomato varieties. Each site and region calls for a slightly different tomato variety. By growing new types each year, you can propagate and share valuable tomato varieties with other gardeners in your area.

Peppers. From sweet peppers to the spicy hot varieties, these warmth-loving vegetables need a long slow summer to flower and produce fruit. Hot peppers range from mild jalapeños to the scorpion peppers that top the scale at 1 million Scoville units, the standard measurement unit for pepper hotness. Whether you slice peppers for salads and cooking, pickle them or make them into salsa—or yearn to challenge yourself with their extreme heat—there are hundreds of varieties from which to choose.

All peppers need a warm, sheltered space in which to grow. That means hoop houses, mini-tunnels, or a full greenhouse for best production. With the right growing conditions, pepper plants return a prolific harvest in a small space. One pepper plant growing in a large pot in a friend's living room is now in its third year, as pretty as a Christmas tree, with living ornaments that are among the hottest peppers to be harvested. In the tropics, or inside our homes, peppers can be grown as perennials.

We start our peppers indoors, planting one seed in each 10-centimetre (4-inch) pot and germinating them under grow lights. Moderate watering is a key to early growth. The plants go through a cycle of potting on to larger pots before they are planted into one of the largest pots in the greenhouse. We transplant one, two, or even three pepper plants into each large plant pot, depending on container size. Placed on a high shelf along the north wall of our greenhouse, they flower, and produce peppers by midsummer. We harvest continually as they produce fruit, to encourage more flowering and fruiting.

When pepper plants are about 20 centimetres (8 inches) tall, they send up a central leader that should be pinched off to encourage branching and maximize pepper production. With more branching, each plant produces many more flowers, and more peppers result. If you provide rich, balanced soil nutrients, the plants develop thick, sturdy stems able to support this heavy production of fruit. Peppers need a steady supply of plant food. Since we grow these plants in containers, feeding with a potassium-rich fertilizer or fish-based tea increases production. We water weekly with diluted fertilizer.

If pepper plants grow more than 30 centimetres (1 foot) tall, support is needed, just as it is for tomatoes. A tomato cage or wooden stake to support the main stem or strings attached to the roof of a greenhouse can provide support. Most peppers, if they are pruned to keep them lower, are self-supporting.

The pepper fruit may change colour as it matures. If you are aiming for red or yellow peppers, wait for the fruit to form and then turn from green to a warmer shade. Red, yellow, and even black peppers are produced from different varieties.

As always, select short-season varieties that grow well in lower temperatures. These varieties are quick to mature, setting fruit earlier and maturing in fewer days. It helps to start seeds indoors, moving them out to a protected space in spring. Feeding plants regularly is essential. But most importantly, warm, sheltered

growing conditions are needed for successful pepper production.

Tomatillos. Called "husk tomatoes" because of the papery husk formed by the flower's calyx, tomatillos (*toe-mah-TEE-ohs*) originated in Mexico and are a staple in green chili sauces in the regional cuisine. Because they grow as a sprawling, weak-stemmed vine, up to 2 metres (6 feet) tall, they benefit from support. The plants have notched, lobed leaves and five-petalled yellow flowers. The fruit forms inside a papery husk that looks like a hanging lantern.

    DAN RUBIN

As with the other nightshades, start these plants indoors, pot them on as they grow larger, then plant them out into the garden once the weather has warmed, under a protective cloche or row cover. Tomatillo vines spread out across the ground, but it is much better to provide netting or staking to keep them off the ground for better air flow and to keep them away from slugs and insects. The growing season ranges from 75 to 100 days. Tomatillos are grown from seed or propagated from stem cuttings.

Favourite varieties of tomatillo include di Milpa, Pineapple, Toma Verde, and Verde Puebla. When harvested, the fruit often has a sticky coating, which washes off easily. To store, keep tomatillos in their husk, and they will last for many weeks, once they are refrigerated. Try making traditional Mexican *salsa verde* by slicing and cooking tomatillos with chilis, garlic, and onion.

Eggplant. *Solanaceae melongena* originated in India or China. A staple in Middle Eastern cooking, it has also become an important part of Italian cooking (think Eggplant Parmesan) and is used in

a variety of Asian dishes. Like other warmth-loving nightshades, eggplants need reliable warmth, full sun, and protection from wind.

Thanks to their broad leaves, these quick-growing plants gain size faster than tomatoes or peppers. Before the fruit develops, the showy flowers add visual contrast. The fruit can reach 22 centimetres (9 inches) or more in length. Most people are familiar with the large, purple-black-skinned eggplants prized in Italian cooking but may not know about the longer types, including striped varieties and miniature forms that are traditionally preserved in curry sauce as pickled *brinjals*.

Start eggplant seeds early, sowing them about 1 centimetre (0.3 inches) deep in sterilized potting soil and germinating them under lights indoors. Transplant to containers or plant out under floating row cover for protection. Pinching off the top sets of leaves encourages growth and better fruit production. Because eggplant prefers slightly acidic soil, do not add garden lime to the soil in which

   DAN RUBIN

they will grow. Suitable companion plants include amaranth, beans, peas, peppers, and spinach.

Harvest eggplant using scissors, slicing cleanly across the stem, to avoid damaging the plant's main growth. Harvesting early (smaller, less mature fruits) gives fruit with more delicate seeds. Mature, full-sized eggplant has a smooth, hard, dark purple to black skin and off-white flesh speckled with dark seeds.

Because eggplant can grow up to 1 metre (3 feet) tall, trellising is needed to support the heavy, hanging fruit. Once known as the "raging apple" or "madde apple," perhaps because of its similarity in appearance to the poisonous plant belladonna, the fruits of *Solanaceae melongena* are delicate and edible.

The full range of forms includes the globe-shaped Italian eggplant; the long, thin Japanese eggplant; Chinese eggplant; Zebra, Little Green; and Rosa Bianca. As with other garden vegetables, try different varieties to determine your preferences and to find those types that grow well in your garden.

22. APIACEAE

Members of the parsley-carrot family (Apiaceae) are aromatic, flowering plants that typically bear flowers in dense, symmetrical circular clusters called umbels. This family has almost 4,000 species worldwide, including dill, parsley, anise, celery and celeriac, carrots, parsnips, lovage, and cilantro.

Celery/Celeriac. These are different cultivars of the same species. Celery is grown primarily for its edible stalk. Celery is a slow-growing annual that requires rich soil, consistent moisture, and effective drainage. It can be challenging for the home gardener, but responds well to optimal growing conditions, with adequate soil moisture, to produce multiple thick, crisp, tasty "leafstalks" used for salads and cooking. Traditionally grown in trenches, earth can be built up around the stalks to blanch them (make them lighter coloured and more tender). Celery thrives when surrounded by mulch and grown under row cover to conserve warmth and moisture and maximize growth.

Celery can be started indoors to give plants a head start, but after they are carefully hardened off, plant them out in a spot with full sun and rich soil, because they are heavy feeders. Planted 25 to 30 centimetres (10 to 12 inches) apart, they will have space to develop a cluster of thick, juicy stems, provided that they have enough food and water for growth. With wide spacing, it is possible to interplant bush beans, arugula, or lettuce as the celery plants slowly grow and mature. Harvest leaf stalks from the outside of the plant, leaving it in the ground to produce additional stalks.

Celeriac, a relative of celery, is grown for its edible stem and root, which has a strong, aromatic flavour. It takes a full 100 days after planting to mature, after which it is dug up, washed and stored in the refrigerator, or buried in damp sand in a root cellar for later use. Recipes that use celeriac include purées, soups, and celeriac cubes cooked in olive oil (Jamie Oliver's favourite) with lemon thyme and sea salt. Oliver calls celeriac "the most underrated [plant] in the whole of the United Kingdom." It is fantastic roasted with root vegetables.

Carrots. Wild carrots (*Daucus carota*, now known as Queen Anne's lace) were originally white, purple, or yellow, not orange. Before Dutch growers developed the familiar sweet, plump orange carrot in the 1500s, carrots were thin and a deep, almost black, purple. Little by little, carrot breeders have refined the colour, selecting for lighter, brighter shades. The prehistory of carrots can be traced back to the time of the dinosaurs, according to researchers at the World Carrot Museum. Carrots are high in natural antioxidants called carotenoids; the darker purple varieties are the highest in these health-promoting compounds.

Carrot seeds form on an umbel (flower cluster), a form familiar to anyone who has grown dill. Carrots produce seed in the second year, if overwintered in damp sand and placed in a cool, dark place. In its first year, the plant develops its thick root to survive through the winter; this root is what we harvest for food. In the second year,

the plant bolts and produces seed, which can be harvested, dried, and saved for replanting.

Because carrots and other members of this family do not respond well to transplanting, seed them directly into the garden. Planting the tiny carrot seeds can be a challenge. You can mix carrot seed with coarse sand, to make it easier to spread them during planting, or buy pelletized carrot seed, in which each individual seed is coated

with a white layer of clay to make it easier to handle. Planting with pelletized seed is easy: simply poke each white seed ball into the soil in a well-spaced, staggered pattern to minimize the need to later thin them out.

Carrot seed can be planted as soon as the ground is warm enough to work. Since it takes up to two weeks for the first feathery leaves to emerge, it is traditional to plant radish seed among carrots, to mature and harvest first. Once radishes are fully grown, they can be pulled, leaving the carrots to form their thick roots. The maturation process for carrot roots can take up to 80 days, so be prepared for three months of weeding, watering, and feeding to produce a healthy crop of carrots.

DAN RUBIN

Carrots grow well in containers if the soil is rich in organic matter, well mixed with sand to make it easier for the roots to penetrate. Although carrots prefer direct sun, they can tolerate some shade during part of the day.

Carrots come in five main types. *Imperator* carrots are the biggest, with narrow shoulders and roots tapering to a fine point. *Nantes* are a popular type, characterized by blunt, shorter roots. *Chantenay,* the best for heavy soils without much sand, are wide at the top but narrow to a point at the bottom; their flavour improves after a frost, late in the year. *Danvers* are large, like Imperators, but better for shallow soils; they grow to 20 centimetres (8 inches) long. There are also *round types* of carrots that are ideal for shallow soils.

Prepare soil to a depth of 30 centimetres (12 inches) by mixing in compost, manure, and sand to create a deep, loose, rich mixture for healthy root growth. About two to three weeks before the last frost, once the ground begins to warm up, seed carrots and cover seeds with a thin (1- to 2-centimetre/0.5- to 0.75-inch) layer of soil.

Intensive planting of carrot seed is fine—as long as they are not too densely planted—since thinning can provide harvests of early, sweet immature carrots for salads. You may become impatient when carrots do not appear a week after planting, and some despair and think that they need to plant again. Be patient: it can take two weeks or even more for the first sprouts to emerge.

As fall turns into winter, the easiest way to preserve mature carrots for later use is to not harvest them. Instead, cover them with a thick layer of grass clippings, maple leaves, or straw, spread a tarp over the mulch, and stake the tarp down at the edges. If you insulate the soil, to prevent freezing, you can harvest carrots all winter. Root vegetables can also be stored in a root cellar or cold room. Carrots placed in bins and covered in slightly damp sand will remain healthy and alive through the winter.

Discourage browsing by deer and rodents by covering carrots with a metal mesh. Carrots are also vulnerable to carrot rust fly. To prevent the fly from laying eggs (which turn into worms that tunnel through the carrot root, turning it bitter) cover carrots with a tent of floating row cover or plant carrots in a box with a lid made from a screen or screen door. These coverings also help retain moisture and warmth, delivering a triple benefit. Once rust fly is in the soil, it can take up to five years for it to be eradicated.

Parsnips. Growing parsnips is easy but requires patience, as they are slow to germinate. Parsnips were once the most widely grown root vegetable in Europe, until potatoes arrived. Parsnips grow best if direct-sown in the garden; prepare the ground the same

     DAN RUBIN

as for carrots. Since parsnip seed is fine and small, seeds can be mixed with sand to space them out.

Thin plants to about 10 centimetres (4 inches) apart. Harvest the roots in the fall, when their flavour will have improved after a first frost. Dig the roots beginning in October, if they were seeded in late spring, or leave some in the ground, protected by straw or sawdust mulch, through the winter. The roots, once harvested, last up to six months if stored in a root cellar in sawdust, leaves, or damp sand, kept above freezing but below 24°C (75°F). Like carrots, parsnips are vulnerable to rust fly. To prevent egg deposit, cover or tent plants with floating row cover, or install a 1.2-metre-high (4-foot-high) screen barrier.

Parsley, dill, anise. These closely related plants are considered herbs: parsley is grown for its leaves; dill, for its leaves and seeds; and anise is a sweeter variation on the same theme.

Parsley is prolific, producing crowns of curly or flat leaves, depending on the variety. Italian or Neapolitan parsley is broad leafed and mild in taste, while its curly cousin is more potent. More than 30 varieties are available. Asian parsley is making inroads in North American gardens; it grows as a perennial and has a strong, slightly bitter flavour. All types of parsley are rich in vitamins A, C, and K and antioxidants, just as carrots are. Leaves can be harvested, dried, and stored for later use, although they do not have the same full-bodied flavour when dried as they do when freshly harvested. Along with its use as a garnish, parsley adds a kick to salads.

Dill, an umbel-bearing herb that grows taller than parsley, needs more protection

from wind and cold and is a flavourful ingredient in pickles, soups, and stews. When dried, the feathery leaves, flowers, and seeds have a more pungent flavour than fresh dill. Dill can be planted in the garden as a companion plant for cabbage and other brassicas, where its distinctive odour repels certain insect pests. Dill attracts beneficial insects, which prey on the pest species. Dill is a favoured species eaten by the caterpillar of the black swallowtail butterfly found throughout much of North America.

Dill can be sown directly into the garden as soon as the soil warms up, or into containers indoors. It prefers slightly acidic, well-drained soil. Once planted, dill sends up a tall stalk, or multiple stalks, ending in umbels, up to 12 centimetres (5 inches) wide. After planting, thin dill to 30 centimetres (12 inches) or more apart, because the plants need space to grow to full maturity. Water well. For a continuous harvest during the growing season, sow seeds every two weeks. If you are growing dill as a condiment to use in dill pickles, let the plant

DAN RUBIN

flower and then go to seed. The seed head is picked and packed into the pickle jar.

Anise produces a cluster of thick stalks and feathery leaves with a distinctive licorice odour and flavour. This traditional medicinal herb settles the stomach and soothes coughs, although we cannot officially confirm its effectiveness. As a flavouring agent, its sweet, aromatic taste is used to make the Greek aperitif *ouzo* and to flavour anisette and other liqueurs. Anise is also added to dairy products, candies, breath mints, and cosmetic products. A favourite in traditional Italian cooking, anise is native to southern Europe, where it has been grown for centuries. Anise is related to star anise, which grows as a tree up to 20 metres (60 feet) tall, and fennel, another member of the carrot family, that is harvested for the thick crown that forms at the base of the leaves.

Growing anise is similar to growing dill. It likes medium pH (6.3 to 7.0) soil, full sun, and regular watering, until plants develop deep roots and are well established. In warmer zones, it is a true perennial,

growing through the winter and producing more leaves each spring. Its flowers feed butterflies and other pollinators. Anise sends up tall stalks of purple flowers that are an attractive visual element in a herb garden or vegetable bed. Like dill, anise reseeds, once the plants mature, making it a reliable self-seeding annual that pops up in the same place, year after year.

Germination takes one to two weeks. Sow directly into the garden after preparing loose, well-aerated soil. Like many herbs, anise grows well in soil with less organic matter. Because anise prefers higher pH soil, add dolomite lime before planting. Anise seedlings are fragile and need protection from wind. Anise can be grown in containers but does not transplant well: seed it where you want it to grow. Plants should be thinned to about 30 centimetres (12 inches) apart. Avoid growing anise near basil or carrots.

Lovage. Less widely known than other carrot family plants, lovage is a pungent, slightly bitter relative of celery prized by some chefs for its distinctive flavour. This plant produces a cluster of large leaves with thick leaf stalks. All parts are edible, including stalk, roots, and leaves, which look similar to celery or flat-leafed parsley. This hardy perennial continues to grow and spread out, year after year.

Lovage is easy to grow. It persists once established, and reseeds without becoming an annoying invasive plant. The Romans grew lovage for its medicinal properties and brought it with them to Britain. The French emperor Charlemagne said it belonged in every garden, while Queen Victoria carried lovage candies wherever she went. In Italy, where it grows as a wild plant, it is called "mountain

     DAN RUBIN

celery." So why is lovage not a common plant in most gardens? Mainly because of its slightly bitter flavour.

Lovage is packed with vitamin C and a cluster of vitamin B-complex compounds and is reported to have anti-inflammatory and anti-oxidant benefits. It is sometimes used to make tinctures and salves.

Lovage needs minimal care once it is established. It can be seeded as soon as the soil can be worked. In winter, it dies back to the ground, then reappears each spring. The stalks, when they emerge, have a slight reddish tinge at the base. Cultivating and feeding around the base of the stalks improve annual growth.

Fresh seed should be used for planting, because older seed quickly loses vitality. Lovage is spread by root division: once well established, the root can be divided to move parts of the plant to new locations. Although slow to germinate (up to 20 days), once the plant emerges, it grows quickly, reaching a height of 60 or more centimetres (2 or more feet).

Cilantro/Coriander: To grow cilantro as an annual, replant it yearly. Put seeds directly into the garden as soon as the soil begins to warm. The seeds are large: space them out. The plants grow well in a sunny well-drained spot. The leaves are used in Mexican-style cooking, while the dried seeds are the spice known as coriander. If you harvest and dry the seeds, you can use them in cooking or replant them, from year to year.

23. ALLIUMS

Members of the genus *Allium* include onions, garlic, leeks, chives, and shallots. Collectively known as "the stinking lilies," they have sought-after flavours and beneficial properties. Garlic, the Chinese saying goes, is "as good as 10 mothers": it can both feed and heal us with its inherent properties.

These earthy, humble roots are actually bulbs, the enlarged base of the plant, which is a storage organ. Alliums are easy to grow and store through the year, if they are well cured after harvest. Here in the soggy north that may mean pulling them out of the ground before the end of August to provide a period of drying out. In the garden, garlic repels insect pests. Alliums like loose, sandy soil, consistent water, and full sun.

Onions. *Allium cepa* is common around the world. Many distinctive strains of onion are grown commercially and in home gardens across the north. Onions selected for long storage include yellow, red, and white varieties. Some are grown to be harvested when small, for pickling, or eaten as greens. Try the sweet onions from Spain and

Bermuda. Short-season varieties suitable for northern gardens include Candy and Stockton Sweet Red.

Some onions do not produce an underground bulb. These "bunching onions" provide some of the earliest crops to be harvested in spring. Whether used in salads or cooked in soups, stews, and casseroles, they provide a pungent boost to the flavour of food. Scallions are mild-tasting, prolific onion greens that can be repeatedly harvested by cutting.

The discovery of "walking onions" at the edges of our garden transformed us into seed producers. Walking onions are a perennial form of giant bunching onion that produces baby onions, known as bulbils, at the top of thick stalks each summer. We grow and market the bulbils as seed stock. Walking onions, also known as Egyptian onions, are worth adding to any garden, for their perennial production of the sweetest, earliest giant onion greens. We harvest the greens (about 2.5 centimetres [1 inch] thick and 45 centimetres [1.5 feet] tall) by late March and have had a fall production of greens as well.

Onions generally need a long growing season and rich soil. Plant seed directly into the garden, or (even better) start seed indoors under lights in early spring. You can also plant onion bulbs, or sets, sold by the bag in many garden stores and nurseries.

Because onions like cool weather early in the season, plant them as soon as the ground warms up, if you are starting with seed. The longer they grow, the larger they become. Whether started from seed, sets, or bulbs, they grow well in raised beds, as well as in mounds or rows in an open garden. They can also be fall planted,

    DAN RUBIN

to overwinter under mulch and emerge with a head start in the spring.

Onions need full sun to reach full size. Prepare the planting site by breaking up hard soil and adding organic matter. Rotate sites for onion planting each year; they are heavy feeders that extract a significant amount of nitrogen from the soil. Another reason to rotate planting location is to avoid diseases that may lurk in the soil. When planting onion sets, do not plant too deeply: they like some sun on the top to help them develop the papery outer layers that protect the bulb during winter storage. Wherever you grow onions, keep the bed free of weeds, as onion plants are easily smothered when young.

Feed onions by watering every week with a diluted weed or compost tea, or diluted fish fertilizer. You can also top-dress with manure or compost. The plants need nitrogen to grow well, so

any way you can add nitrogen during the growing season should be used. Once bulbs begin to form, light mulching with grass clippings or straw helps the bulbs retain moisture. Make sure that they get enough water: check the soil to see if it still damp, 5 centimetres (2 inches) down and deeper.

Thrips and maggots are persistent pests that attack onions, but they are not usually a problem in the north, where winterkill takes care of them. Unless the soil is extremely wet, problems with mould during the growing season are unlikely. Well-drained soil deters mould.

Summer or fall harvesting of onion bulbs should allow sufficient time for effective drying for winter storage. Wait for the leaves to fold over, indicating that growth has stopped. Then pull the bulbs. Do not wash them. Let them dry and cure in the sun, then brush off the dirt. Curing onions requires exposure to sun on a dry surface, deck, or screen, for up to a week. After that, hang them in a cool dry place for further drying. If the climate is too wet in the fall, cure them indoors with a dehumidifier running to properly remove moisture.

We have regularly lost onions, when braided and hung from the ceiling in our warm, moist kitchen. David Goodyear has advised us to avoid this by harvesting earlier, trading onion size for better storage. He recommends harvesting in August, rather than waiting until the fall to pull and cure onion bulbs.

DAN RUBIN

Garlic. Ah, garlic, the stinking rose! What a wonderful plant, especially if you like the resonant spicy smell of garlic cloves. Whether in chili and garlic sauce (a condiment used in Asian cooking), incorporated into Italian sauces, or roasted in the oven until tender, garlic provides a foundation for great meals all around the world. We agree with Nova Scotia garden guru Niki Jabbour that garlic is an essential crop in northern gardens.

Garlic comes in two types. Soft-necked garlic is ideal for spring planting and easy to braid for hanging and storing; hard-necked varieties are planted in the fall to overwinter and appear the following spring. Soft-necked garlic is generally better suited to warmer climates—but with suitable enclosed protection, both types can thrive in the north. Hard-necked garlic grows much larger than soft-necked garlic if planted in rich soil with lots of compost but produces fewer cloves per bulb than soft-necked garlic. Each clove, wrapped in papery skin, clusters around a central stalk.

Some varieties produce white sexually reproductive flowers that turn into black shiny seeds. Other varieties are sterile, with no flowers; these produce vegetative bulbils at the tip of a flowering stalk. These bulbils are genetic clones of the parent plants and can be saved and replanted, but they must go through two years of growth as individual bulbs before splitting to create the multi-clove bulb that is more familiar and desirable.

Planting fall garlic is simple. Break individual cloves free of the garlic stem—keeping the paper skin on—and poke them down into holes in the soil with the pointed end up and the flatter side (where

the roots form) below. Plant with the tip 5 centimetres (2 inches) below the surface of the soil to shelter them from winter frost. We cover the entire bed with a 22-centimetre-thick (9-inch-thick) layer of maple leaves for an added layer of insulation. The maple leaves break down the following year and feed the soil. We seal the bed with a plastic tarp laid down over the maple leaves and stapled to the edges of the raised bed. As soon as the soil begins to warm in the spring, we peel the tarp off. Then up come the garlic leaves, poking through the dry maple leaves, but still sheltered beneath their thermal protection. This method has produced garlic bulbs as big as a fist each fall.

An important early garlic harvest are garlic scapes, the flower stalks that form on garlic stalks in midsummer, curling around in preparation for setting flowers and forming bulbils. Once the scapes have formed a complete circle, we cut or break off the stems.

Garlic scapes are prized for their tenderness and exquisite flavour. Although almost as pungent as garlic bulbs when fresh, the flavour mellows as soon as the scapes are cooked. We stir-fry them in olive oil with tamari, sea salt, and a splash of balsamic vinegar. We also harvest and pack 15-centimetre (6-inch) lengths of scape into sterilized jars, fill the jars with vinegar, water, salt, and spices and place them in the refrigerator, where the pickled scapes last for months and add a tangy treat to meals.

Harvest and store garlic the same as for onions. Do not wash garlic after harvest; washing can introduce mould spores into the bulb's core. Instead, cure them in the sun, wipe off the dirt, and dry them for up to two weeks, hanging them, bulbs downward, indoors. We built a garlic rack to hang from the rafters in our shed, allowing us to thread the stems of the garlic between parallel slats, where they hang, upside down, all winter.

It is a challenge to dry garlic fully, and more than once we have lost a portion of our beautiful garlic to mould over the winter. The key to preserving garlic is effective drying after harvesting, followed by storing in a cool, dry place. Hanging the garlic bulbs in our shed, where the temperature occasionally drops below freezing in winter, is a good solution: the garlic bulbs, rich in oil, resist freezing.

Among the best varieties of hard-necked garlic for northern climates are Music, Spicy Ukrainian, and Purple Stripe. Unless a local supplier provides your garlic bulbs, we recommend Vesey's, a seed house in Prince Edward Island, our favourite Canadian source for seed garlic. In the US, seed garlic is available from regional suppliers, including High Mowing Seeds in Vermont. In recent years, with a surge of people returning to gardening, seed houses have sold out early, so order fall-planted hard-necked garlic bulbs by early spring.

The fall harvest of garlic, whether soft- or hard-necked, is both food and seed stock for fall planting. If you consistently replant the largest, hardiest bulbs, you will join in the ancient tradition of creating locally adapted plants. The garlic trims to local conditions as it survives and adapts, year after year.

Leeks. Leeks are another easy-to-grow allium, favoured for their hardiness, mild flavour, and array of uses. The thick stalk is made up of layered leaves that grow taller as they add layer after layer, never forming a bulb below ground. As the leaves thicken, they grow out from inside the plant. Soil can become trapped between these layers. Leeks are traditionally planted in a trench, then backfilled with soil to blanch once the stems have been hidden below the ground.

Start leeks indoors in February to March, then transplant them into the garden in early spring. It is easy to tease apart the roots of a thick mat of tiny leek plants after starting them indoors. Leeks are an efficient plant to start indoors; they are hardy and easy to transplant.

Replant individual leek seedlings in a row or trench, setting them about 7 to 10 centimetres (3 or 4 inches) apart, then covering their roots with soil and watering them with diluted compost tea. They continue to grow taller and thicker throughout the summer.

Leeks are a cool-season biennial plant. This cold tolerance is a gift to northern growers. Planting in trenches, in addition to blanching the leaves, creates additional protection as the weather grows cold. Leeks prefer soil with a pH between 6 and 7 and they grow well in rich, organic soil. As they have shallow roots, do not let the surface soil

     DAN RUBIN

become dry. On the other hand, too much watering, especially if they are planted in a trench, can cause mould. Two centimetres or so (1 inch) of rainfall or watering per week is enough. When you do water, make sure that more than the surface is wet by probing a finger into the soil to determine that moisture has penetrated below the surface. When weeding around leeks, do not damage the shallow roots that spread out in all directions. Once the seedlings are well rooted, a growth spurt will occur. After they mature, they can stay in the ground, right through the winter, and be available for harvest. To protect leeks from snow and ice, mulch or tent them; they can survive even when the ground freezes.

Leeks can be simmered in soups (particularly cream soups), stir-fried, cooked in casseroles and quiches, and are used in a wide range of other dishes that put their subtle onion flavour to good use. Thoroughly clean leeks before cooking, as dirt can become trapped between the layered leaves.

Preferred varieties of leeks for northern growing include the large-sized Musselburgh, as well as Bandit, Tadorna, Chinook, and King Richard, a favourite for its smaller size and productivity.

Chives. Chives are a type of bunching onion that produces clusters of thin dark green leaves and then papery white to purple flowers, during the summer. Grown as a perennial, they spread and reseed to new spots, but they are easy to control—remove the new plants, if you do not want them to spread. Both decorative and useful as food, chives are a delicate, showy, plant that forms thick dark green bunches 30 centimetres (12 inches) in diameter if allowed to grow from year to year. Chives can also be grown in

indoor or outdoor containers. Permaculture teaches us to keep one pot each of chives, oregano, thyme, rosemary, and sage growing outside the kitchen door for easy use.

A hardy perennial, chives can be seeded indoors and kept moist until they germinate. Seeds respond well if the soil is slightly warmed with a heating mat. Once they are growing, they can be planted out as soon as the soil can be worked. They will continue to divide and spread, so it is often easier to separate and move clumps to new locations than starting them from seed, unless you try a new variety. Chives love full sun but are slightly shade-tolerant. To harvest chives, grab a cluster of leaves and cut them at the base with scissors. The missing leaves will quickly be replaced by new growth.

Garlic chives, also known as Chinese chives, are a different species with a garlic flavour. These are easy to grow and well suited to container growing. Garlic chives are not as cold-tolerant as the common variety of chives. Their leaves are flatter and lighter green and grow as tall as 10 centimetres (4 inches). They have white, rather than purple, flowers and are ideal for indoor growing.

Shallots. Shallots are a variant of onion that originated in Asia, then travelled through India to reach the eastern Mediterranean in prehistoric times. Their name comes from their association with the city of Ashkelon in Israel, from which the ancient Greeks believed they came. They are closely related to multiplier onions that also grow in tight clusters.

Shallots contain iron, copper, phosphorus, potassium, magnesium, and manganese, as well as high levels of certain vitamins. They are an important source of selenium, which helps humans form antibodies to resist harmful bacteria and viruses.

Most gardeners grow shallots from bulbs purchased in a nursery, garden store, or supermarket. They can also be grown from seed. Planted in the fall and overwintered, they grow best in full sun

     DAN RUBIN

with well-drained, rich soil. Like onions and garlic, they are heavy feeders, needing an adequate supply of nitrogen for full growth.

I was recently given a bunch of large shallots by a friend who keeps chickens; it was clear that the nitrogen in the chicken manure accounted for the size of these shallots. Feed shallots nitrogen-rich fertilizer. If shallots are planted late in the fall, they remain dormant over the winter, then begin to grow again with warmer weather in the spring, and are available for harvest by summer. Spring planting produces a later harvest.

Plant shallot cloves about 15 centimetres (6 inches) apart. They like slightly acidic (pH 5 to 7) soil and require a dormancy period during which they are cooled to just above freezing in order to start growing. Shallots prefer well-drained soil. They tolerate soil with low nitrogen, but with the addition of compost or other nitrogen-rich material, they grow much larger.

Shallot varieties for northern growers include Ambition, Conservator, French Red, and French Gray, considered to be the heirloom variety most true to type. Another variety to consider, if you can find bulbs or seed for it, is Frog's Leg, an heirloom with a mild flavour and an elongated shape reminiscent of a frog leg.

Shallots are ready to be harvested about three months after planting. It is best to dig up the whole plant, shaking off excess soil but never washing them, to avoid mould. They can then be placed in a cool, shady spot outdoors or indoors to cure. That takes a few weeks. After curing and drying, they can be braided, hung, or have their roots and tops removed for storage.

24. LEGUMES

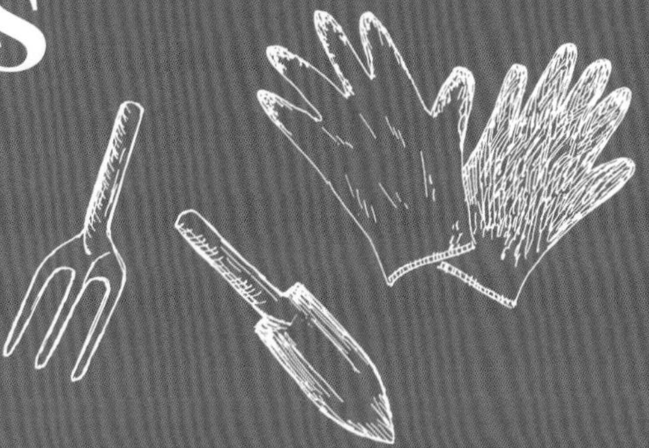

Peas, beans, and their relatives—the legumes—are a source of edible, storable protein. They are easy to grow and are well suited for colder climates. They add nitrogen to the soil, thanks to the nitrogen-fixing bacteria that cluster in symbiotic nodes along their roots. The Fabaceae, the legume family, includes annual herbaceous (leafy) plants along with some trees, vines, and bush varieties. They are a large and economically important group of flowering plants.

We are most familiar with the peas and beans growing in our gardens and on farms. Generically called *pulses*, peas and beans are part of the legume family, with more than 40,000 varieties cultivated and growing wild. Pea plants generally have a hollow stem, while the stems of most beans are solid. Both peas and beans produce pods holding their seeds after they mature and flower; these seeds are valued as a food source for humans and other animals. In dried form, pulses can be stored for years, for replanting or for use as food. Rich in protein and easy to cook, they can also be sprouted or eaten raw, delivering an intense boost of nutrients.

Planted in a sunny spot in well-drained soil, the roots of legumes harbour colonies of bacteria that absorb nitrogen from the air and fix it in a form that plants can use. This makes legumes a valuable crop for restoring soil fertility. Planting peas or beans after a heavy feeder such as onions, garlic, or squash is a very practical idea.

Various types of peas and beans have found their way into a range of regional food traditions, from steamed green peas to baked beans to the fava beans that are a staple in Middle Eastern cooking. Growing them gives us food that can be dried and stored and can also connect us with a diversity of world food traditions.

Peas. Garden peas are climbing vines that send out curly tendrils to cling to whatever they can find for support. Pea vines can grow 2 metres (6 feet) or more and need physical support. As they grow, the stems sprout leaves and the flowers that will turn into seed pods once they are pollinated by insects.

Pea varieties are specialized for different seasons: some produce an early-season, some a mid-season, and some a late-season harvest. Succession planting can extend pea production through the summer and into the fall.

Try planting three basic types of peas: shell peas, to harvest the green peas that form inside pods; snow peas, that produce crisp, flat, immature pods used in traditional Asian cooking; and sugar snap peas, a relatively recent creation that will maintain tenderness, even when the pod is full-sized. Developed in the 1970s, snap peas can be harvested before the seeds are fully formed and plump and used in the same way as snow peas.

All three types are great for picking and eating fresh. Although harvesting and shelling peas is tedious, it is an activity that connects you intimately with your food as you remove the peas from the pods and then steam and serve them. Green peas are at their best prepared as soon as possible after they are removed from the pod.

DAN RUBIN

Planting peas too early is a common gardening mistake. Wait until the soil is warm to the touch and well drained. The large wrinkled, dried pea seeds are perfect for introducing gardening to children and other beginners. One caution: some legumes sold for seed have an anti-fungal coating to help them survive in damp ground. If pea seeds are coated with a pink layer, that coating is toxic and should not be handled without gloves. If you plant without gloves, wash your hands with soap and water immediately after planting.

Once planted, pea seeds will germinate if the soil is warm—but there are ways to get a head start on the growing season. One option: soak dried peas for several hours in warm water, then place them in the dark in a closed container or in an open dish covered with damp fabric or paper towel. Check them daily. Once the seed has split and the root has begun to emerge, they are ready to plant. Alternatively, start them by planting into containers filled with potting soil. Transplant within days after the first stalks appear, to avoid crowding the roots.

Once a bean or pea germinates, the root forces the seed up through the soil surface, then the cotyledons (seed leaves) spread, breaking through the seed coat, and the true leaves start to grow. We have seen crows pulling sprouting seeds out of the soil, thinking them edible, then discard them when they see the roots, hop along the row, and pull out the next one down the line. Discourage this practice by installing a scarecrow or something that flaps in the wind, such as an aluminum pie plate hung from a string.

Whether you are planting unsprouted dried seeds, sprouting seeds first, or transplanting pea plants already growing in soil, you

can sprinkle inoculant (available from a local garden store) onto the soil and stir it in to provide a starter for the nitrogen-fixing bacteria that allow the pea plant's companions to gather nitrogen from the air.

Peas prefer well-drained soil and a sunny location. Once mature, they capture their own nitrogen for fertilizer, but it is worthwhile to provide rich, organic soil to start them. Work some manure or compost and dried, crumbled seaweed into the soil before planting. Since peas prefer slightly alkaline soil, add 1 cup dolomite lime for every square metre (10 square feet) to raise the pH.

Pea vines are vigorous climbers, gaining several inches per day during the warmth of summer. While some dwarf varieties are essentially self-supporting, most peas are vines that can climb up

    DAN RUBIN

strings, a trellis, or netting. Build a system of support, either before you plant or immediately afterward. The seed packet should state the maximum height, but in general—and because not all labelling is accurate—you should build a trellis at least 2 metres (6 feet) tall. Various designs, using slats of wood, netting, or fencing, can provide the needed support.

We poke pea seeds into the soil about 5 centimetres (2 inches) apart, in a double, staggered row. The vines do not take up much space, since they grow vertically; spacing them close together helps increase production. After a week or two, plant again for a succession of harvests through the summer. For extra-early production, try planting a more compact bush type that matures earlier. Peas can also be planted into a planter box, placed on a deck or in the garden, and protected against frost with a hood of floating row cover early in the season.

Once pea plants begin to climb, they are generally hardy, but if a week without much rain occurs, you should soak them deeply with

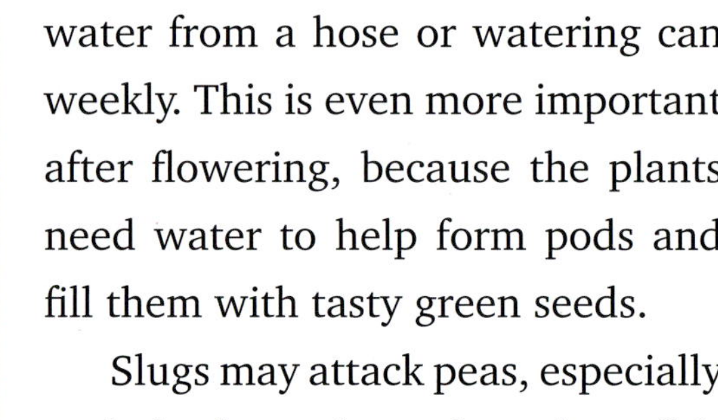

water from a hose or watering can weekly. This is even more important after flowering, because the plants need water to help form pods and fill them with tasty green seeds.

Slugs may attack peas, especially early in the spring, when the soil is damp. Other than slugs and snails, few pests interfere with the growth and flowering of peas in the north.

Our favourite way to check whether peas are ready to harvest is by picking and eating them while wandering through the garden. Pea plants sense when they have successfully produced seed; if you do not harvest the ripe pods, the plants will shut down production. But if you harvest steadily from the ground up, pea plants will continue to produce new flowers and pods.

Our favourite varieties of peas include Lincoln shell peas, Dakota dwarf peas, Knight early dwarf peas, Thomas Laxton early peas, Mr. Big mid-season peas, Dalvay mid-season peas, Oregon Sugar Pod peas, Sugar Lace snow peas, and Sugar Sprint short-season sugar pod peas.

Chickpeas, also known as garbanzos, are another common legume, well known from their use in Middle Eastern cooking, where they are ground up with sesame seeds and oil to make hummus.

     DAN RUBIN

Chickpeas are also a main ingredient in various dishes from India. Chickpeas need three months of growth to produce well, so they may not be suitable for all northern gardens. Starting them indoors helps extend the growing season, but it can take up to two weeks for them to germinate. Do not soak the seeds before planting. The roots are delicate: transplant with care. Chickpeas like slightly lower pH soil, between 6 and 8, full sun and rich soil, with good moisture retention.

At the end of the growing season, add dried pea vines to your compost or dig them into the soil to retain the benefits of the nitrogen that the root nodules have captured. Winter-planted legumes such as vetch, and other nitrogen-fixers including buckwheat and winter rye, offer other ways to return nitrogen to the soil.

Beans. Like peas, beans are nitrogen-fixers, thanks to the bacteria that grow in nodules along their roots.

A traditional garden practice developed by the Indigenous growers of Central America, called the "Three Sisters," involves planting beans along with squash and corn, so that squash plants can spread across the ground, and beans grow up the corn stalk, while adding nitrogen to the soil. Beans, like peas, need support as they climb, unless they are the bush varieties that grow and produce pods closer to the ground.

Bean seeds can be dried and stored for later use, but we also grow varieties to be harvested and eaten fresh. Seed catalogues list hundreds of well-known beans as well as heirloom varieties. If you are looking for the wild and unusual, order the catalogue published by Baker Creek Seeds. In that inch-thick volume, appropriately titled *The Whole Seed Catalogue*, you will find metre-long beans from Taiwan, Chinese python snake beans, Japanese winged beans, purple pod beans, and giant Golden Butterwax beans originally developed by American growers in the 1890s. This vividly demonstrates the amazing range of beans that can be grown by home gardeners.

Pole Beans. Climbing beans are collectively known as pole beans. Our favourites include Kentucky Wonder (a thick-fleshed green bean also known as Texas Pole beans) that produce large, fleshy pods that are tender until they swell to full size. We have also grown Painted Lady, a variation on the well-known Scarlet Runner, setting bright flags of red and white flowers that turn into large, thick pods. Other varieties that thrive in the north include Kentucky Blue, Carminat, Rattlesnake (with green and purple pods) and Maxibel, a French filet variety.

Because these varieties each have a growing season between 55 and 70 days, they are well suited to northern propagation. But there are many others to choose from. As you search through seed catalogues, or as a member of Seeds of Diversity, you will discover a whole world of beans. Pay close attention to the length of season to determine which ones will thrive where you live.

     DAN RUBIN

Bush Beans. Bush beans do not require support; they branch out rather than climb and produce flowers and seed pods closer to the soil. As with peas, dig compost and manure into the ground, add dolomite lime to raise the pH, and then plant directly into the ground. Bush beans can be spaced as close as 15 centimetres (6 inches) together in rich soil; if planted closer, it will be difficult to comb through the packed plants to find the ripe pods, especially if they are green rather than yellow or purple.

To make spacing easy, lay out the individual bean seeds (either presoaked or dry) in a staggered pattern across the bed, then poke them down into the prepared soil, 2.5 to 5 centimetres (1 to 2 inches) deep. Orientation of the seed is not important, since the root that first emerges and the growing shoot that follows will find their way regardless of orientation.

Bush bean varieties ideal for northern gardening include Purple Queen bush beans, Jacob's Cattle beans, Gold Rush wax beans, Taylor dwarf beans, and a wide range of green bush beans, including Provider, Mascotte, Romano, and Landreth Stringless. These will not all be found in one catalogue, so the hunt for the best bean can be an excuse to order even more seed catalogues and browse a wider range of sources!

Fava beans, also known as broad beans, produce a large, flat seed that is a favourite in Middle Eastern and Greek food. They are popular in Britain and Spain. Their enormous pods can grow up to 30 centimetres (12 inches) long and produce seven flat green seeds that dry white, once harvested. *Vicia faba* is closely related to vetch, a wild vining plant that is grown by farmers as a nitrogen-fixer. One caution: for some people, fava beans trigger G6PD, a hereditary enzyme deficiency, which can lead to anemia. If you experience discomfort after eating fava beans, get genetic testing for this deficiency.

Other popular beans include lima beans, a flat type also known as butter beans or Madagascar beans, that share the same caution as that stated above for fava beans. Lima beans are popular in a range of recipes in which they are prepared in rich sauces with longer cooking, which smooths out their dry, sandy texture (as kids we called them "sandbag beans"). Named for the capital of Peru, lima beans need warm soil to grow well and come in both pole and bush bean forms.

"Potato limas" are a pole bean that can grow up to 4 metres (12 feet) tall. They tolerate some shade but need soil that is at least 18°C (65°F) to grow well. Unless planted in a warm, sheltered, sunny spot, they may not be suited to growing in a northern garden.

Start bean seeds in the same way as for peas. They can be dry-planted into warm soil, sprouted first, or planted indoors early in the spring and set out later. Transplanting beans into the garden is tricky because of their delicate roots; if you start them indoors, treat the roots with care as you settle them into the garden and gently pack soil over the roots. In many ways, it is easier to direct plant

     DAN RUBIN

bean seeds than pea seeds, because beans are more tolerant of cold, damp soil. But wait for the soil to warm to at least 15°C (60°F) before planting, for best germination.

If you plant more than a dozen bean plants of any variety, be prepared for a hefty harvest. In addition to cooking pods whole, they can be left on the plant for the bean seeds to mature, for late harvest and dry storage. If the beans are true breeding (OP, not hybrid), consider saving seed for the following year. But because beans are pollinated by insects that fly a long way, longer isolation distances are critical to keep bean varieties from hybridizing. If more than one type of bean is grown side by side, order new seed each year to ensure consistent varietal production.

Stretch out the harvest by planting several bush bean and pole bean varieties more than once. Some varieties can be grown mainly for dry harvest; others, for eating or cooking when fresh. If you are overwhelmed by the tidal wave of mid-season production, pickle some beans.

Pickled beans are easy to prepare. Pods should be washed, stems removed, and then slow pickled in brine, or packed directly into jars and quick-pickled with hot vinegar, water, salt, and spices and placed in the refrigerator to mature. For longer storage, sterilize jars of pickled

    DAN RUBIN

beans in a water bath canner with canning jars fully immersed in boiling water for 20 to 25 minutes. Once sealed, they keep for years. If beans, or any other vegetable, are not pickled or canned in an acid solution, they must be pressure-canned at a temperature above 80°C (176°F) for a minimum of 20 minutes, to eliminate botulism.

Bean plants are susceptible to mould, rust, and other fungal diseases as well as bacterial blight. Brown lesions on the leaves indicate fungal impact, while bean rust shows as raised brown or yellow spots on the leaves. Fusarium is a form of root rot caused by a fungus. By using certified seed, planting resistant varieties, and changing the location in which you grow beans from year to year, these problems can be avoided.

In general, overwatering or planting in soggy, compacted soil will increase the chance of plant diseases. Well-drained soil with high organic content protects and keeps plants healthy. Adding mulch around the plants minimizes weed germination and improves soil health.

25. ASPARAGUS, ARTICHOKES, SUNCHOKES, SWEET POTATOES

Our survey of common garden vegetables ends with four oddballs. Botanically, they are not related, but they have in common the ability to add additional flavours and variety to your food supply, although they may be more challenging to grow.

Asparagus. Originally a Eurasian coastal species, *Asparagus officinalis* now grows as a naturalized plant across western Canada by the sides of streams as well as in home gardens. Asparagus shoots are harvested before the stem turns into a bushy, fernlike mass of thin branches. Although asparagus can be grown from the seeds that form inside little green balls as the plant matures, it is generally planted in the form of root clusters, called crowns.

An asparagus crown looks like a dried-out octopus, a mat of tapering roots bundled together and attached to the stub of a single stem. That is the dormant asparagus plant. Plant this crown into a deep bed enriched with layers of manure and mulch that will feed and protect the plant as it grows.

Before planting, soak the crowns overnight in water or compost tea. Dig a large hole in the garden bed, leaving a fist-sized mound of rich soil in the middle. Gently separate and spread the roots of the crown, draping them over the sides of the mound. Cover the roots with fresh soil. The top of the crown should be about 7.5 centimetres (3 inches) below the surface of the soil. Space the next crown at least 22 centimetres (9 inches) away, and continue planting in a wide, staggered pattern.

Asparagus can take up to three years to produce an adequate crop because the roots must first become established, access sufficient nutrition, and spread out to produce multiple stalks. Once the stalks emerge, the familiar form of a spear of asparagus will be recognizable. Cut spears at the base once they are about 22 centimetres (9 inches) tall. A new stalk will replace it. You can harvest multiple times from a mature crown, but always leave at least one stalk to create the bushy fernlike plant needed to capture sunlight and feed the roots.

Cover the asparagus bed with a thick layer of mulch every winter to protect the tender plants and help them survive. Even with a 22-centimetre-deep (9-inch-deep) layer of compost as winter mulch, it can be challenging to grow asparagus. Every year we plant a few more crowns, hoping our asparagus will root. Asparagus thrives near running water and does not mind extra soil moisture; for best results, creating warm, moist, well-drained soil is the goal. Peaty soil can lead to root damage. To create the best growing conditions, add lots of manure and compost to the soil, digging down 45 centimetres (18 inches) between established plants to enrich the soil all the way down to the buried roots.

Rather than growing asparagus in rows or in a raised bed, create an "asparagus patch" where this perennial wonder can thrive, feeding itself and providing delectable asparagus shoots during a six-week harvest. If they are gathered early, new shoots for a second, late-summer, harvest will form.

DAN RUBIN

Artichokes. According to a woman who sat beside me on a flight across the Pacific many years ago, "the choke of the artichoke is the joke of the artichoke, but the heart of the artichoke is the art of the artichoke." She could not have better captured the paradox of consuming the unopened flower of a giant, domesticated thistle. Along with cardoons, another thistle relative, the wild artichoke was only recently brought into cultivation during the Roman Empire, in contrast to many other plants that were domesticated many thousands of years earlier.

The artichoke's scientific name, *Cynara*, has its roots in Greek mythology: the god Zeus at first made the girl Cynara a goddess, then turned her into a thistle after she deceived him. Artichokes were discovered and domesticated along the shores of the Mediterranean. Even though they come from a warm, dry climate, they are now grown widely in the Middle East and on the central

coast of California. Propagating them in the north requires some patience, but it is possible.

We select the variety Tavor as the best for our growing conditions. While most varieties take two years to mature and form a flower, Tavor will produce artichoke buds in the first year. In late winter (February/March), we set the small, round seeds in sterilized soil and germinate them under lights. Once they sprout and have set their first leaves, we transplant them to larger containers, then water and feed them.

About two weeks after the last hard frost (mid-May), we transplant the seedlings into an outdoor bed of rich soil, and water them weekly with compost tea. In dry weather, daily watering helps. Planted in rich soil and well protected with mulch, the plants produce flower stalks in July or August. By late summer or early fall, the unopened flower buds are harvested for a few excellent meals of steamed artichokes served with garlic butter.

Overwintering requires maximum protection; 9-centimetre-thick (6-inch-thick) mulch and an enclosure or tent over the plants will protect the roots. Low pH soil (5.6 to 6.6) and lots of compost or well-rotted manure as top dressing keep the plants producing throughout the growing season.

Sunchokes. The Jerusalem artichoke is not an artichoke and did not come from Jerusalem. Now known as sunchokes, these tall, skinny sunflowers produce a delicious, crisp, starchy underground tuber. Sunchokes are invasive, so they must be contained to keep them from taking over the garden.

We isolate sunchokes in raised beds and harvest the roots (which look like gnarled gingerroot) in late winter or early spring, after

DAN RUBIN

the frost has caused them to turn sweet. They are one of our most reliable early harvests. Wash the tubers and thinly slice them for eating raw, grate into salads, or bake, roast, or steam them. When cooked, they become soft and are easy to purée for dips and they can also be used to thicken soups and stews. Their flavour is reminiscent of that of artichokes, which may account in part for their name.

Plant sunchoke tubers about 22 centimetres (9 inches) apart and 5 to 7 centimetres (2 to 3 inches) deep in the soil in early to late spring. They come up slowly, then grow taller to take the form of closely packed sunflowers. Their small, attractive blooms range from pale yellow to deep red, depending on the variety. Several types are grown in local community gardens and backyards in our province; ask around to see if you can find seed stock for your own garden.

We highly recommend sunchokes, as long as they are not allowed to invade your garden. Once established, they spread and are challenging to remove. But as a reliable, high-production, low-effort perennial, grown in a raised bed or other enclosed space, they are an invaluable food source.

Sweet potatoes. You may not think that sweet potatoes, a plant better suited to warmer climates, would grow well in the north, but with enough warmth, they can survive and produce edible tubers, if provided with the right growing conditions.

Closely related to morning glory, *Ipomoea batatas* is a creeping vine that produces dark orange underground tubers with dark brown skin. Roasted or boiled, these starchy roots become sweet. The shoots and leaves are also edible. Originating in Central and South America, sweet potatoes may have crossed the Pacific centuries before Europeans arrived, based on new information from genetic studies of similar plants found on Pacific islands. They became part of our food supply even before being carried across the Atlantic to Europe by Columbus.

Growing sweet potatoes in the north requires a technique that we learned from Tim Livingstone of Strawberry Hill Farm. His family farm grows sweet potatoes and other crops just outside Pembroke, New Brunswick. Beginning with either organic sweet potatoes or commercial ones purchased at the grocery store, bury the tuber in a tray or plant pot

Sunchokes are a tall sunflower that produce a starchy, edible root.

DAN RUBIN

in damp soil. Place the tray in a warm room under lights and keep the soil moist. In about six weeks, sprouts will emerge and grow toward the light. When the stalks are at least 15 centimetres (6 inches) tall, break off each sprout from the original sweet potato. Unless you do this, they will not develop new tubers.

Dip the sprouts in rooting powder (crushed Aspirin is a good substitute) and plant with their base in rich soil in individual pots. Once they have developed a mat of new roots, the seedlings can be planted out. To produce new sweet potatoes, plants need rich soil and consistent warmth. Whether grown in a greenhouse, in deep containers, or planted outdoors under floating row cover, they must be protected from cold, wind, and frost. As the vines spread, cover them with soil and heavy mulch. Livingstone harvests his sweet potatoes in the fall and stores them in refrigerated containers for sale to customers.

Our experience with growing sweet potatoes has been mixed: our plants did produce tubers, but they were thin. We concluded that it is possible to grow sweet potatoes here in the north, but they must be well protected from cold. The folks at Northern Homestead in Alberta have also grown sweet potatoes, starting with slips ordered from seed companies as well as grown from commercial sweet potatoes.

26. GRAINS AND PSEUDO-GRAINS

All civilizations rely on some form of storable food. For the earliest urban empires—the pyramid builders of the Middle East—that meant wheat and rye. For centuries of Chinese dynasties, the staple grains were rice and wheat. For the Incas, it was potatoes, quinoa, and maize. Grain lies at the heart of civilization, as food and as the basis for fermented beverages.

Whether consumed in the form of beer, bread, or porridge, or cooked and eaten with vegetables, meat, or fish, grains are our primary source of carbohydrates, energy foods that have allowed humans to build empires, expand into new landscapes, support expanding populations, and conquer their neighbours through invasion and war.

If your goal as a gardener is to move your family toward self-sufficiency, or if you just like the idea of growing and milling your own flour, you may be interested in cultivating the grasses and other plants that produce grain and seeds that are like grain. Because of the storability and general usefulness of grains, planting them can extend your reach as a home food producer.

Growing grain requires a series of complicated and challenging steps after harvest: threshing (removing the hard outer husk of the grain) followed by winnowing (separating seed from chafe). After that, the seeds must be ground or milled to produce flour.

Maize. Known in North America as corn, this popular, large-seeded grain made its way across the Atlantic during the Columbian Exchange, then travelled back to North America, where it is now grown for food, fuel, and animal feed. Corn, in various forms, is now a major part of our diet.

For northern gardeners who wish to grow corn on the cob, the

     DAN RUBIN

essentials are planting short-season varieties and protecting plants from blasts of wind and cold. We have had success starting corn plants indoors with seeds planted in small individual containers. Once they sprout, the plants can be hardened off, then transplanted outdoors into a raised bed. A separate pollen grain is needed for each corn kernel to form, so the best method is close planting of no more than 20 centimetres (8 inches) apart

Because maize is shallow-rooted, wind can actually tip over a whole planting or bed of corn. A fence or chicken wire cage surrounding the bed or plot will help support the corn stalks so that they can remain upright and resist blasts of wind.

Harvest cobs when they are mature, checking first by peeling back the husks of one or more ears. The best advice we have heard about how to cook corn is to have the water already boiling, or your roaster prepared, before you even pick the corn.

Seed selection should focus on short-season varieties. New "peaches and cream" bicoloured types (hybrids) are available every year from local seed houses. These types actually become sweeter after they are picked, as their starches are converted to sugar.

Wheat. Although originally domesticated in the warm, dry climate of western Asia, wheat has been adapted to grow in a range of regions, including northern China (where wheat replaces rice as the staple grain crop), Ukraine, western Europe, and the Great Plains of North America. Emmer, an ancestor of wheat, was first grown as a cereal crop more that 12,000 years ago along the eastern edge of the Mediterranean. As mutant forms were noticed and selected by farmers, the plant and its seeds have increased in size. Wheat is now grown on more hectares around the world than any other crop.

Here in the north, the key is to find varieties of wheat and other grains that are well suited to short-season growing. The varieties sold as winter wheat are one option. Planted as a cover crop, frost-tolerant winter wheat survives through dormancy in the coldest months. If planted in the fall, it will overwinter and come up the following spring to produce grain in the second year. Some varieties of winter wheat can survive in temperatures as low as -15°C.

Rye. Winter rye, a cover crop used by farmers to put fertility back into the soil, is also a reliable food crop grown for centuries in northern Europe and Russia, where rye bread (made with a mixture of rye and wheat flour) is a traditional staple. Growing rye offers the advantage of combining a winter cover crop with one that produces edible grain, if left to form seed heads in the second year.

Rye is easy to grow. Plant it by hand broadcasting, seeding it thinly across a large area, then lightly till or rake the seed in. Planted in the fall, it sprouts with wet weather and grows even as the weather turns cold. When planted as a cover crop, it is normal to cut it or plough it in, in preparation for summer planting. But for grain production, allow it to flower and form seed heads that can be harvested in late summer or the following fall. Rye needs little care but requires regular rainfall or irrigation to produce well. It is ready to harvest when the leaves look dead and have turned yellow brown.

Once seed heads turn golden (or dark brown), cut them off and store them until they are fully dry. Traditional ways to remove the seed casings include walking on the seed heads or beating them with sticks. If you have harvested a small amount, rolling the seed heads between your hands or passing them through the rubber rollers on an old wringer washer (if you can find one) separates the seeds from their casing. The result: a mixture of seeds and chaff. After that, tossing to remove chaff is one way to winnow the seeds, although a bit harder than with the lighter chaff of wheat. However, separating seed from seed head is easier than with the harder seed casings of wheat.

Barley. A cold-hardy grain, barley tolerates almost any climate, including short growing seasons and cold winters. It prefers a cooler

     DAN RUBIN

climate for ripening but will not grow if the ground is too wet. Two types of barley (two- and six-row) are grown. On its own, it does not have enough gluten to create the elastic dough that allows bread to rise, but can be mixed with wheat flour to make barley bread.

Oats. Oats are well suited to northern cultivation. They are generally planted in spring and harvested in the fall. The introduction of hull-less oats makes harvesting much easier than for oats with hulls that must be threshed and winnowed to remove the seed covering. Plant oats by hand: seed over an area of dry, well-drained soil, then rake in the seeds to keep them out of sight from birds. Water regularly in dry weather. Seeds heads need only about 45 days after planting to ripen.

Harvest oats once the seed heads are golden brown. If left to become dark brown, they may split and drop seed on the ground.

After air-drying for a week, thresh seeds (by spreading them out on a clean sheet or tarpaulin and walking on them, or hitting them with a blunt wooden paddle or bat) and then winnow them to remove the chaff. Fully dried, they can be stored for many months, and ground into flour or cooked as a cereal.

Triticale. A modern cross between wheat and rye, triticale is higher in protein and lower in gluten than wheat. Although it is grown mainly for livestock, it is also used as a winter cover crop.

Ancient grains. This term is a generic label for a collection of semi-wild grains. These ancestors of modern wheat attract attention among holistic farmers because of their nutritional benefits and lower gluten levels: they include emmer, spelt, einkorn, and pseudo-cereals such as buckwheat, quinoa, and bulgur.

Millet. Millet is the name for a group of small nutritious grains produced by four different genera of grasses. Millet seed heads resemble corn tassels. Millet has a nutty flavour and its grains are rich in niacin and the antioxidant beta carotene. It tolerates both damp and dry soils, but the soil must be at least 16°C (60°F) before planting in the spring. Millet is generally harvested in October. Plant individual seeds about 7.5 centimetres (3 inches) apart. It is ready to harvest after 60 to 70 days of growth. After harvest, roll millet grains between metal rollers or crack them with hammers to remove the covering. This step makes processing millet difficult for the home grower.

Buckwheat. Sometimes referred to as "the northern grain" because of its popularity and ease of cultivation in northern Europe and long history in northern Russia, buckwheat is not a grass but a member of the same family as sorrel and rhubarb.

Its seeds form within a hard, angular casing, making it easy to grow but difficult to harvest, since the tough outer seed covering must be cracked to free the seeds for eating. Commercially, this step is achieved by running seed casings between metal rollers. Like some other grains and legumes, buckwheat attracts bacteria that cluster on its roots to capture nitrogen from the air. Buckwheat is therefore valuable as a cover crop, but is also grown for food.

Sow buckwheat groats (seeds) from late spring to early summer in a sunny, well-drained location. Plants put up flower stalks crowned with white or yellow flowers that form seed clusters once fertilized. Buckwheat thrives in cool weather. It tolerates acidic soils and can be used to improve soil conditions, since it is a nitrogen-fixer. Locating seed for food-grade buckwheat can be challenging, since it is mainly cultivated in North America as a cover crop. If you have a local Co-op store, check with them for seed.

Amaranth. The family that includes quinoa and the wild plant

known as pigweed or lamb's quarters is closely related to spinach, as well as the flower known as love-lies-bleeding. In addition to wild pigweed, which is an excellent food source (as explained in chapter 32), it is possible to grow quinoa and red amaranth for their edible seeds, commonly sold as an alternative to wheat and other grains.

This pseudo-grain originated in Mexico; the Aztecs called it *huahtli* and used it for ceremonial purposes. Renewed interest during the 1970s made quinoa popular because of its high fibre and protein content. Because amaranth does not produce gluten, it has become popular as an alternative to grain in whole foods. Amaranth grains can be popped like miniature popcorn and the leaves steamed or sautéed.

     DAN RUBIN

Cold-tolerant, easy-to-grow varieties of amaranth are available to northern, short-season growers. Once established, amaranth is drought-tolerant, and the plant does not need a lot of nitrogen in the soil.

Amaranth grains are the plants' seeds. They germinate in temperatures of 13°C (55°F) and plants grow up to 120 to 150 centimetres (4 to 5 feet) tall. The seeds can be sown once it warms up, or started indoors in late April, hardened off, and planted outdoors once the weather is warmer. Because the genus *Amarantha* includes more than 50 species, finding a zone-specific adapted variety is a challenge. Some are grown as decorative plants: the huge, plumed variety "elephant head" is grown for its upright burgundy seed heads that resemble an elephant's trunk, with plumes of harvestable seeds.

Seeds for Burgundy amaranth, Strawberry Fields, Globe amaranth, and several other edible varieties are available from High Mowing Seeds in Vermont, while Vesey's in Canada supplies seeds for a large flowering amaranth called Century Mix Celosia, grown as an ornamental. Richters has Grain amaranth and the Canadian company McKenzie Seeds sells the seeds for Red Leaf amaranth. With a light application of compost, these varieties grow well in colder climates.

Our friend Dan Jason, owner of Salt Spring Seeds, is an advocate for northern grain growing. As he stated in an article in *Small Farm Canada*: "For those of you who have had any experience with gardens, be assured that grains and cereals are the easiest crop to grow and they are extremely rewarding." Contact Prairie Garden Seeds, based in Humboldt, Saskatchewan, for more information, and to obtain seed for northern grains.

27. BUSH FRUITS

Even though we live in an exposed, windy, coastal location, we have had good fruit production from our trees, shrubs, bushes, and vines. Fruit production is both possible and important as a garden element. The key is selecting the right varieties and planting them where they will have the soil and shelter that they need. Once established, except for annual feeding and pruning, these plants are easy to maintain and harvest.

Strawberries. Low-growing leafy plants that like acidic, sandy, well-drained soil with lots of mulch, strawberries send out runners—long, extended stems that develop a cluster of leaves and then re-root in a new location. The name strawberry comes from their preference for growing in straw mulch, which protects the plants and keeps their fruit away from the damp soil. Mulching with straw, wood chips, or sawdust is recommended.

When starting a strawberry patch, add a 20-litre (5-gallon) bucket of sand and at least the same amount of compost or manure to the soil and mix it in well before planting. Strawberry plants are

usually sold in bunches that have been harvested and tied up, 12 to 20 at a time. Before planting these dormant crowns, soak the bundle in water or compost tea for several hours, then separate the individual plants. Each plant will have a cluster of leaves attached to long thin roots. To plant them in a prepared bed, dig a broad, shallow hole, fan out the roots, and cover them with 5 centimetres (2 inches) of soil, with the leaves just above the soil's surface. Space strawberry plants 23 to 30 centimetres (9 to 12 inches) apart. Once established, the plants develop a wider crown of leaves and fill in the space between the plants. Every summer they send out runners, long thin stems that sprout to become new plants.

Periodic feeding with compost tea or diluted fertilizer that contains phosphorus encourages fruit set. Strawberries are either June-bearing, everbearing, or day neutral. June berries have one short season of fruit production; the other two continue setting fruit through the warm months. All three die back and become dormant during the winter; heavy mulching helps them survive frost and cold.

Bred originally from alpine strawberries that produce tiny full-flavoured fruit, the modern strawberry sets fruits that are 2.5 to 5 centimetres (1 to 2 inches) thick. The best berries retain the sweet, tart flavour of their smaller ancestors. Woodland strawberries, among the day neutral types, are closer to the ancestral form. They reproduce by seed, do not produce runners, tolerate some shade, and produce fewer, smaller berries. There are many varieties of wild strawberries from which to choose.

     DAN RUBIN

Strawberries thrive in raised beds because drainage is generally better there than at ground level, and the soil warms earlier in the spring. Strawberries are also suited to container and vertical gardening: you can guide the runners to new containers or locations to create new plants. Remove plants that are older than three or four years and keep the new ones created by their runners.

Strawberries begin flowering in mid-May or later in a colder year, and by early summer should be setting fruit. As the berries turn from white to pink to bright red, they may need protection from flocks of birds: cover plants with netting. Slugs can be a problem (so, as suggested in chapter 15, protect the berries). Maintenance through the year includes pinching off flower buds for the first few weeks to delay fruit set, weeding to remove aged plants, thinning by removing runners, directing some runners to establish new plants in gaps left in planting, and covering plants with a carpet of mulch 15 to 23 centimetres (6 to 9 inches) thick in the fall.

Some varieties of June-bearing plants recommended by the University of Minnesota, where work is being done on cold-climate fruit production, are Annapolis, Jewel, and Cavendish, while a preferred ever-bearing type is Ogallala.

Blueberries. The wild blueberries that grow on bluffs beside the sea and along rural pathways here in Atlantic Canada are second to none for their concentrated flavour. The wild low-bush variety bears fruit low to the ground. They are a focus for family foraging in late summer and early fall, when berry pickers spread out into the hills and park along the highways to gather them. These berries are exceptionally sweet and tasty, with a more intense flavour and higher levels of antioxidants than the cultivated types.

Even though they are not well suited to commercial production, wild blueberries are easy to harvest and are delicious in pies, jams, and jellies or frozen for later use. We recognize that they are not well adapted to home cultivation but are a beloved wild plant, best suited to annual harvest where they prefer to grow.

Some varieties of low-bush berries have been developed for commercial production and researchers continue to work on crosses between low and high bush, but at present there is no reliable source for a promising hybrid.

High-bush blueberries are woody, perennial shrubs that grow up to 2 metres (6 feet) tall or even higher but they need to be pruned back to make them easier to pick. Look for a northern-adapted variety such as Blueray, Jersey, or Patriot. High-bush blueberries produce fruit that is larger than the wild ones, but not as flavourful. They lend themselves to commercial cultivation as well as fruit production in a home garden. They can be started from cuttings, but most gardeners buy high bush plants from a commercial source. Growing several varieties improves flower fertilization and berry production.

Currants. Currants produce reliable fruit in a cold, northern climate. Plant perennial white, red, and black currants if space is available toward the back of your property. Even though they may be cold-hardy, plant currants in a sunny spot, sheltered from the dominant wind, for better growth and increased fruit production. Because currants grow in damp, boggy soil, they are an ideal choice for areas that are unsuitable for other crops.

Black currants were once banned in parts of the US because they were thought to carry a fungus that affects white pine trees, but new, mould-resistant varieties have made them popular again. They have significant potential for use in juices and wine making— we produce up to 40 litres (10 gallons) of wine each year from our black currant bushes. They are known to be rich in antioxidants and

    DAN RUBIN

good for health, in general.

Currants originally came from northern Europe and still grow wild in Siberia. Although they can be started from seed, it is best to obtain currant bushes by division of well-rooted stands. Because they grow so well, they tend to take over; many of our neighbours and friends are happy to have us remove plants. In this way, we have steadily added black currant bushes to our garden each year. Prune old wood annually to maintain healthy bushes.

Red currants grow in much the same way as black and white currants, on a bush that spreads out, sending up new shoots every year. Their berries glow like crimson jewels when we harvest them. Red currant jelly has the same brilliant bright red colour.

Gooseberries. These plants, closely related to currants, grow very well in the north. Like currants, they produce fruit on tall stems that are equipped with wicked spikes. Their German name is

stachelbeere, which means "stab-berry." We think of this each fall as we endure repeated stabbings from their long, sharp thorns, while harvesting them.

Like currants, these berries form on second-year wood, so encouraging new shoots and removing old canes is a good practice. The tart, striped fruit can be up to 2.5 centimetres (1 inch) in diameter, although some varieties are smaller. We harvest our gooseberries after they have turned dark purple and sweet, but some prefer picking them when they are still light green and tart. They have a distinctive, musky odour that adds a flowery fragrance to jams, jellies, and wine.

The best way to introduce gooseberries into a garden is by taking cuttings from existing plants, rooting, and then planting them in a spacious location. Use low rails to contain the tall canes to make it easier to harvest the fruit. Gooseberry-currant sawfly is a major pest when it appears, skeletonizing leaves in a few days. The sawfly infestation will not necessarily last from year to year.

Raspberries. Raspberries are another cold-tolerant bush fruit, familiar in both their wild and cultivated forms. Plant raspberry canes in a location where they can spread or plant in rows, enclosed by a fence or trellis. They produce berries on second-year wood; maintenance involves removing old canes and feeding plants with compost and layers of mulch. Containing rows with rails makes them easier to harvest. Growing raspberries from cuttings is the best way to introduce them to a garden. Raspberries range from golden to bright pink and red and come in many varieties. The fruit is soft and best suited for home gardening, since shipping and handling can be difficult. Recommended varieties for northern growing include

     DAN RUBIN

Boyne, Encore, Nova, Anne, and Royalty.

Haskaps. Native to northeast Asia, this relatively new plant to North American gardens produces small, lozenge-shaped purple-black fruit. Haskaps are a member of the same family as honeysuckle. They are native to circumpolar countries, including Canada, Japan, Russia, and Poland. They are also called *honeyberry,* perhaps in recognition of their relation to honeysuckle.

Haskaps grow best in slightly acidic soil and full sun but tolerate partial shade. They expand to become thick, bushy plants, so plant them 2 metres (6 feet) apart, giving them space to grow. The fruit's firm texture is reminiscent of kiwi; its tart flavour has been compared to a mixture of raspberries and blueberries. The original strain, imported from Siberia, has been further developed by the University of Saskatchewan to create three commercial types: Tundra, Borealis, and Indigo Gem. Although they take a few years to become established and produce fruit, haskaps are easy to grow. They are not self-fertile, so you need to plant two or more varieties close together for effective pollination.

Grapes. Many people think grapes will not grow north of the Canadian border, but in fact, from British Columbia to the Niagara Peninsula of Ontario, as well as here in Atlantic Canada, commercial vineyards are thriving. Some varieties will survive and produce fruit in the north, if they are well protected from cold and wind, even in Newfoundland and Labrador and the colder northern US states. The key is to plant the right varieties.

If you do not have a greenhouse, locate grape vines in a sunny sheltered spot protected from the wind. Our outdoor grape vines are more than eight years old. We have planted several different varieties that bear harvestable fruit each fall. These grapes, planted originally as an experiment in challenging the climate, include a few from local plant nurseries and two from regional seed houses.

For harvesting full-size table grapes, greenhouse growing is recommended. We have used grapes from three varieties of our outdoor plants for wine making: Lucy Kuhlman, Minnesota 78, and Valiant, all well adapted to the north. Other northern varieties include Himrod, Beta, Marquette, and Louise Swenson. Since grape vines tend to spread out, trellising them on horizontal wires maximizes fruit and facilitates harvesting. Annual pruning encourages growth and concentrates fruit production.

Kiwis. Consider Northern or Arctic kiwis for northern fruit production. Because male and female plants are necessary for fertilization, at least one of each is needed. Growing as vines up the side of our back deck, these northern kiwis have yellow-green leaves, edged in red, then they set flowers and produce fruit on the female plants. The small, light green fruit are not as large as commercial kiwis imported from New Zealand and marketed widely in North America, but they are very tasty. Plant northern kiwi vines in a sunny place where they can climb a trellis or against the south-facing side of a house. Arctic kiwis are exceptionally hardy and wind-tolerant.

Rhubarb. Although not a berry like the other plants recommended in this chapter, rhubarb stalks are used in the same way as many berries, to produce jams, jellies, pies, and wine, so we include rhubarb here.

Rhubarb is a member of the genus *Rheum*, native to China and Russia, where it has been grown for centuries and used for food and medicine. Around 1770, it showed up in England—seeds were likely smuggled in—and was then grown commercially. It spread across the Atlantic from there.

The root and leaves are poisonous because of the presence of high levels of oxalic acid, but the stalks are edible and prized for their intense sour flavour. Growing rhubarb is easy: it thrives in damp ground and spreads out to create an intense cluster of thick stems and broad leaves if provided with a good source of nitrogen. Top-dress with manure, fish waste, or compost every year for a thriving rhubarb patch. Annual feeding in the fall is recommended.

People debate whether to harvest the stalks by cutting or pulling them. We believe either way is fine, and the plant will continue to produce more stalks. Remove the off-white flowers and flower stalks when they form, to support more leaf stalk formation.

Rhubarb can be used in jam, pastries, and other ways, sweetened to balance the sour taste. We make rhubarb wine, which is easy to do by combining rhubarb chunks with sugar, water, and yeast.

Rather than planting rhubarb seeds, you can easily separate a chunk of root from the original plant and transplant it. Rhubarb is a low-maintenance crop that just needs a place to grow and lots of nitrogen to feed its roots.

28. TREE FRUITS AND NUTS

Two major families of fruit trees—*drupes* and *pomes*—have been developed over centuries by humans, from wild trees that bore tiny, almost inedible fruit to become dietary staples and sources of flavour and carbohydrates.

Drupes (also known as stone fruits) include cherries, apricots, plums, peaches, nectarines, almonds, loquats, and olives, closely related plants that produce fleshy fruits formed around a single seed encased in a hard, woody covering. This family also includes coffee, coconuts, and mangoes. In northern climates, the most familiar are cherries, apricots, plums, and damsons. Blackberries and raspberries (chapter 27) are aggregate drupes.

Pomes are multi-seeded fruits encased in a fleshy covering, derived from flowers with multiple carpels or seed-forming sections. Pomes are part of the rose family (Rosaceae), and include apples, crabapples, pears, and quince. Apples originated in the area around Kazakhstan, pears in southeastern Europe, and quinces in the eastern Mediterranean.

Reliance peach is the best variety for northern gardens.

Before commercial production began to dictate which varieties we eat, more than 17,000 named types of apples were cultivated in North America. *The Ghost Orchard* by Helen Humphreys describes how apples were brought from Europe and then spread across North America over the centuries. Many were grown in Indigenous village orchards until westward expansion displaced the Indigenous residents, as colonial settlers evicted them and took over their land. In the Annapolis Valley of Nova Scotia and on the Pacific northwest coast in Oregon and Washington, apple orchards still produce thousands of pounds of fruit.

Start with grafted trees. Although some gardeners have had success starting fruit trees from seed, this is not a reliable way to produce fruit, because successful production depends on a careful selection of fruit variety and tree size. Most fruit trees that are sold have been grafted: they combine root stock selected to determine tree size and cold tolerance with grafted fruit wood selected for the type of fruit the tree will produce.

Starting a tree from the seed of an apple or plum offers no guarantee that the tree will resemble either parent, survive, or be of a practical size. You will not know if the tree is successful for many years, until it shows how well it grows and what fruit it produces. When establishing a home orchard, it is best to plant professionally grafted trees.

Tree sources. Size becomes important if you do not have room for a full-sized apple or cherry tree. A dwarf or semi-dwarf variety is easier to prune and harvest. Smaller trees take fewer years to begin producing and are less vulnerable to wind damage. Because root

     DAN RUBIN

stock determines cold tolerance, look for types that grow well in your location and climate. It is best to purchase trees from a reliable source focused on cold-tolerant northern varieties: for example, Hardy Fruit Tree Nursery in Quebec, Whiffletree Farm and Nursery in Ontario, and Corn Hill Nursery in New Brunswick. The University of Minnesota has become a centre for development of northern fruit varieties, while the University of Saskatchewan is also developing cold-tolerant varieties, including bush cherry varieties.

Avoid multi-grafted trees. The fruit trees sold at big box stores may be grafted to as many as three or four varieties of fruit. It is tempting to imagine a single tree providing all these types of cherries or apples. However, trees that have been multi-grafted likely will not grow well in a challenging northern setting for which they have not been adapted. Rather than starting with a tree that has already been multi-grafted, it is better to plant a single variety and graft later, once the tree is well established.

Planting. We have learned several important things about planting fruit trees from Stefan Sobkowiak, an accomplished permaculture orchardist based in Ontario. Many home gardeners put their trees into a hole and then fill the hole with a dense mixture of compost or manure. This is a mistake: the new soil will retain water, which can cause the roots of the young tree to drown. For good drainage, it is best to fill the hole with the same soil that came out of it.

Plant fruit trees in locations protected from strong winds. As our dominant wind comes from the northwest, we plant to the southeast, in the lee of a tree or building, so that the strong wind is blocked or deflected past the tree.

Dig a hole twice as large as the root ball of the tree or the pot in which it was purchased. Remove the tree from the pot and unwrap the burlap in which the roots may have been bundled. Use a hose to wash away the soil around the roots and assess if any have been

damaged or crossed. Remove or prune away broken or crossed roots to create a fan of major roots to support root growth.

In the bottom of the hole build up a central mound of dirt. Lower the tree into the hole, centring it over the mound, and splay the roots in a fan over the mound. While holding the tree upright, return the dug soil to the hole, gently tamping it down around the roots then filling the hole to ground level. The graft must be at least 5 centimetres (2 inches) above the top of the soil: it can become an entrance point for disease if it is buried in the soil.

In an exposed, windy location, help new trees survive by wrapping the tree in burlap during the winter to reduce the drying of buds and branches. Once the tree is well established, with a strong root system, this is not necessary. Wrapping the trunk with chicken wire can help prevent browsing by snowshoe hares and deer.

Feeding trees. Rather than adding fertilizer to the bottom of the hole around the roots, apply fertilizer, manure, and compost on

top of the soil, around the base of the tree. As rain and irrigation water dissolves the nutrients, they slowly sink into the soil. Do not place plant food close to the tree trunk: this signals to the roots that they do not need to reach out to find nutrients. The tree needs a strong root structure. Over time, as the tree grows, its branches reach out and its roots mirror this growth underground. Feed the tree just outside the drip line, below the outer limit of the branches, where the fine root hairs search for nutrients.

Annual mulching around the trunk is recommended to reduce the need for weeding and to layer slow-release nutrients on top of the soil. Sobkowiak no longer fertilizes the fruit trees in his orchards; instead, he plants nitrogen-fixers such as sea buckthorn, alder, legumes, and buckwheat beside each fruit tree to provide essential nitrogen.

Each major fruit crop requires certain growing conditions.

Apples. Our 11 apple trees provide a bountiful fall harvest from which we make applesauce and pies along with fruit that we keep in cold storage during the winter months.

Apple varieties were once selected for specific use in pies, juice, or applesauce, or for winter storage. The tradition of the winter apple, hard and starchy when harvested that gradually ripens and turns sweet after being picked, is almost lost to current knowledge.

Rather than planting a single apple tree, people would plant a small orchard including at least one of the main types used for cooking, juicing, winter storage, and eating fresh.

Grocery-store apples are now selected and grown to look appealing after months of cold storage and long-distance shipping. What is generally sold as "apple juice" is a diluted concentrate that is stored in tanks, then reconstituted, flavoured, and recoloured, rather than fresh, unfiltered juice rich in pulp and flavour.

You can press your own apple juice if you have the space for enough juice trees. We have crammed more than 20 fruit trees into our double-wide city lot, selecting semi-dwarf varieties to save space. If you have an acre or more, a small orchard becomes more feasible. But do not plant the standard store varieties! Instead, seek out heritage types, selecting for flavour, scab resistance, and suitability to the cold north.

In Canada, producers such as Sheridan Nursery graft and grow out trees, then ship them bare rooted in bundles, to local nurseries where they are potted, proofed, and sold to farmers and home gardeners. If fruit trees are ordered bare root, starting them in containers will make sure that they are healthy and ready to plant. We prefer to leave this work to trained horticulturists, knowing that we will receive a healthy tree, ready to plant, in the late spring. We plant fruit trees after the last hard frost to give them a cycle of warm weather to become established and well rooted.

Here are some apple varieties recommended by horticulturists Todd Boland and Ross Traverse:

     DAN RUBIN

- *Britegold*: developed in 1980, a bright red and light green disease-resistant cross
- *Cortland*: a 1915 cross between Ben Davis and McIntosh, a popular variety
- *Cox's Orange Pippin*: striped English variety that may require warmer conditions
- *Dayton*: relatively new bright red apple with yellow flesh developed in Indiana
- *Freedom*: developed in the US, released in 1983, scab-resistant
- *Greensleeves*: a favourite from England, yellow at maturity
- *Honeycrisp*: developed at the University of Minnesota, crisp and flavourful
- *Liberty*: released in 1978, disease-resistant, suited for immediate eating
- *Murray*: a Canadian scab-resistant McIntosh cross

- *Northern Spy*: tart, stores well, ideal for pies
- *Novamac*: developed in Kentville, Nova Scotia, and released in 1978
- *Prima*: scab-resistant eating variety grown since 1958
- *Redfree*: disease-resistant red and green eating apple from Rutgers University
- *Richelieu*: a medium-sized apple developed in Quebec
- *Rouville*: Canadian apple developed in 1962, greenish yellow with red blush
- *William's Pride*: crisp, juicy, slightly spicy bright red apple, can be late harvested
- *Yellow Delicious*: a flavourful tender-skinned apple, ideal for baking

DAN RUBIN

If this list is confusing, consider that Whiffletree Farm and Nursery in Elora, Ontario, offers 21 different northern apple varieties, while Wikipedia features an annotated list of thousands of known varieties, with 7,500 types of apples still being grown around the world.

We recently learned from fellow gardener David Goodyear that apples fall into four different groups that need to be matched up correctly for effective pollination. In general, a good pollinator for apple trees is a crabapple or an apple tree from a different variety.

Crabapples. While these smaller apples may not seem as useful as full-sized ones, they attract pollinators and their diminutive fruit can supply the pectin needed to set jams and jellies.

Crabapples are also grown as decorative flowering trees; if you plant these for food, make sure that it is a variety that sets fruit. Crabapples make a delicious jelly when cooked down and mixed with sugar or honey. Because of their high pectin level, they are among the easiest fruit to use for making jelly. Prized for their fragrant blossoms and fruit that turns deep red in the fall, crabapples are a suitable foundational plant in the landscape. For northern gardens, recommended varieties include:

Flowering crabapples

- *Spring Snow*: a white flowering variety
- *Prairie Fire*: red blossoms
- *Pink Spires*: pink, of course
- *Centennial*: red blooms

Crabapples for fruit production

- *Rescue*: sweet taste for fresh eating, red fruit, readily available
- *Trailman*: sweet green and red fruit, for fresh eating and cooking
- *Dolgo*: bright red fruit, tart taste, suitable for jelly, readily available
- *Early Yellow*: plant hardiness zone 1, small yellow fruit, hard to find
- *Red Siberian*: small red fruit, hard to find, suitable for jelly
- *Norhey*: plant hardiness zone 1, green fruit, hard to find
- *Osman*: plant hardiness zone 1, reddish fruit, hard to find

Because crabapple trees can grow up to 8 metres (25 feet) tall, plant a crabapple in a place where its shade will not interfere with sunlight reaching the rest of the garden.

Pears. Pears date from the Bronze Age in Europe, and even earlier in China and the Middle East. Pears do not store as well as apples, but they can be eaten fresh, canned, and baked. Because pears tolerate wet soil, take advantage of this when choosing where to plant a pear tree, to make the best use of all the areas in your garden site or property. Planting generally follows the same process described for apples.

Hardy Fruit Tree Nursery offers a selection of pear varieties that are well adapted to northern conditions, including Julienne, Loma, Lorraine, Nova, Patten, Siberian, Southworth, Summercrisp, and Vekovaya.

According to the Hardy Fruit Tree website, as long as winter temperatures do not drop below -47°C (-53°F), pears can survive, even in zone 2, which includes Saskatoon, Regina, Edmonton, Winnipeg, and Thunder Bay. In addition to being a reliable fruit for colder climates, pears are generally insect- and disease-resistant. Other than Flemish Beauty, a European variety which is sensitive to fungal disease, many varieties maintain healthy growth without any treatment.

Harvesting pears at the right time is critical. If left to ripen on the tree, they become mealy. They are ready for harvest when they begin to blush with colour but are still hard. Refrigerate harvested pears. A few days before eating them, remove them from refrigeration and they will soften and sweeten. Press the top of the fruit beside the

stem; when the flesh is slightly soft, they are ready to eat.

Some pear varieties are self-fertile; others require a companion tree of another variety for pollination and fruit production. Plant more than one pear tree, placing the second nearby to aid bees and other pollinators in connecting the two trees.

Quince. Although not as well-known as apples and pears, quinces are an ancient pome, grown for both flowers and fruit. Like crabapples, quinces have a high level of pectin and are valuable as a gelling agent for jams and jellies.

Quince trees produce beautiful, fragrant flowers. Prized for their blossoms, flowering Japanese quinces (*Chaenomeles japonica*) form spiny hedges about 2 metres (6 feet) tall, although they are slow growing. A second type is the tree quince (*Cydonia oblonga*), which grows to 8 metres (25 feet) and produces golden yellow fruit. The fruit of both species is woody and inedible before being cooked.

Other types of quinces produce sweet, edible fruit with a flavour reminiscent of that of pineapple. These can be cooked down to make sauce or fruit butter with a rich flavour. The English word *marmalade* comes from *marmelo,* the Portuguese term for quince, in tribute to the rich, spicy flavour that this small, yellow fruit adds to jams, jellies, and pies.

Quinces prefer rich, well-drained soil and full sun. Layer compost and manure around the tree trunk after planting, and every year after that. Quince trees tolerate soggy soil but grow better and more quickly

    DAN RUBIN

in a well-drained site. Mature quince trees can grow up to 3 metres (10 feet) tall and spread their branches out just as wide. Give them room to grow without shading out other plantings. Although quinces grow well in warmer settings, they are well adapted to northern growing, especially Meech's Prolific Quince, Vranja, and Rea's Mammoth.

Cherries. Some varieties of sweet and sour cherries do well in northern gardens. Our Queen Anne trees produce as much as 13 kilograms (30 pounds) of ripe cherries each year. It will take many more years for our Montmorency sour cherry trees to reach full maturity and produce harvestable quantities of their tart fruit, ideal for pies and jams.

Among the commercial cherry varieties developed at the Canadian research station in Summerland, in the Okanagan Valley of British Columbia, are Cristalina, Lapis, Satin, Sentennial, Skeena, Sovereign, and Staccato.

As with other fruit trees, root stock determines mature tree size. When planting, consider that a full-sized cherry tree may exceed 3 metres (10 feet) tall and take up to five years for cherries to come into full production. As a purchased tree is already three or four years old, expect fruit production to begin after a few years and increase as the years pass. Feeding cherry trees by top-dressing with fertilizers, compost, and manure directly below the drip line keeps them

healthy and increases fruit set. Hand pollination expedites this: break off a branch with flowers from one tree and use it to dust the flowers on another cherry tree of the same variety.

The University of Saskatchewan has released three strains of bush cherries that produce large quantities of fruit on relatively low, bushy plants: Crimson Passion, Juliette, and Romeo. These bushes are cold-hardy and handy for picking because they are closer to the ground. Plant more than one variety of bush cherry for cross-pollination, even though they are self-fertile.

Apricots. Our northern climate is generally too harsh for most apricots. But some cold-hardy varieties grow well, particularly in a greenhouse with a tall roof: select the right variety, with root stock for a smaller size if you wish to fit in an apricot tree. Like other fruit trees, apricots require a period of cold dormancy to produce fruit.

Apricot varieties for colder sites include Canadian White Blenheim, Chinese Semi-Dwarf, Goldcot, Moorpark, Puget Cold, Tilton, and Tomcot. Although some research may be required to track down these trees, the effort is worthwhile if the planting site is well sheltered from dominant winds and deep snow.

Plums. Plums are well suited for northern gardening since they originated in the mountains of central Asia and Turkey. Traces of cultivated plums have been found at Neolithic (New Stone Age) sites. By the time of the Roman Empire, more than 300 varieties were being cultivated. About 18 plum varieties are currently grown commercially. The home gardener must decide between European and Japanese plum varieties: each offers unique characteristics. Black knot resistance is an important factor when choosing plums.

We thank Dan Kinzler, a horticulturist at North Dakota State University's Extension Service, for the following list of northern plum varieties:

- *Alderman*: burgundy-red skin and sweet flesh; vigorous tree flowers heavily; zone 4
- *Black Ice*: large, dark blue fruit with sweet reddish purple flesh; naturally dwarfed; zone 4
- *LaCrescent*: small, yellow, sweet and aromatic fruit on a vigorous tree; zone 4
- *Mount Royal*: produces fruit even if it is the only plum tree but does not pollinate others
- *Pembina*: large, red-skinned oval fruit; delicious yellow flesh is sweet and juicy
- *Pipestone*: large red fruit; tough skin peels easily to reveal sweet golden flesh
- *Superior*: dark red with firm yellow flesh of outstanding, super-sweet quality; zone 4
- *Toka*: small to medium, dark red skin; rich and spicy flavour; outstanding pollinator
- *Underwood*: red skin with golden flesh; ripens mid-August with a long fruit season
- *Waneta*: large fruit, yellow skin with red blush; sweet and juicy yellow flesh

Kinzler advises that plums should be planted in full sun and need at least six hours of direct sunlight. They should be planted after all danger of frost has passed. Place each tree at least 4 metres (12 feet) from neighbouring trees. Because their branches spread out, plums are ideal for creating a privacy screen at the edge of a property.

Plum trees produce sprouts (suckers) from the root stock; remove these to avoid competition with the grafted fruit wood. Yearly pruning keeps the centre of the tree open and healthy. Annual fertilizing with compost or a well-balanced fertilizer is also advisable. If birds damage and pick the fruit, use netting to keep them out. Wrap the tree trunk with burlap or another form of insulation in winter.

Damsons. Damsons (*Prunus institia*) are a separate species from plums that have naturalized in New England and the Atlantic provinces. Damsons resemble purple plums but are smaller and do not have the characteristic indented plum seam. Damson stones are easily removed—which is not the case in true plums, which have juicier flesh. Because they are drier, damsons are preferred for baking, while regular plums are better for preserves and jams.

Damsons can be planted from seed, rather than grown from grafted stock, or they can be grafted to plums, to which they are closely related. However, these fruit-producing trees suffer from black knot, which can make them difficult to grow.

Peaches. Few people in Newfoundland and Labrador would think of planting a peach tree; but it is possible to harvest peaches if the right variety is planted. Like the other stone fruits, peaches grow best in well-drained soil, full sun, and a longer summer.

Two varieties are sufficiently cold-tolerant for northern production: Red Haven and Reliance. Of these, Red Haven is more likely to suffer from peach leaf curl, a fungal disease, if exposed to cold rain and snow during the growing season. Reliance is the preferred

DAN RUBIN

variety; we have harvested dozens of large, golden fruits from this type of peach tree at maturity. Reliance peach trees can survive cold weather because they are grafted to root stock from the Himalayan foothills. Released in 1964, this self-fertile peach produces large, yellow-skinned peaches with a reddish blush.

The essentials for peach tree growth and production are rich soil and shelter from wind and cold. Plant in a sunny, well-sheltered spot, protected from the dominant wind by a building or a larger tree. Make sure that the graft is above ground. Dig a hole twice as large as the root ball, plant, and fill the hole with the same soil that was dug out, for good drainage. Newly planted fruit trees need to be watered regularly to encourage root growth. Soak them weekly, particularly in dry summer weather.

Various tree nurseries in the US and Canada graft Reliance peach trees and provide them to local nurseries. An online search will identify a regional source.

Nut trees and shrubs

While nuts may not be the first food crop to come to the northern gardener's mind, growing nut trees and bushes is possible if the right kinds have been selected. Here are some types to consider. Because these are perennials, once established they will become a steady source of annual production, with little maintenance needed.

Hazelnuts. Also known as filberts, hazelnuts are produced by shrubs that grow well in colder climates. Mature hazelnut bushes each fall produce clusters of nuts, each one sheltered within a fibrous cup-shaped husk. As the nuts begin to fall, about seven months after flower pollination, they can be harvested or gathered up after they fall to the ground. Hazelnuts are a valuable source of oil, protein, and vitamins.

These prolific, easy-to-grow nuts are disease-resistant and tolerate a range of conditions. By hybridizing native varieties with those from Europe to produce larger nuts, agricultural researchers have developed several cold-tolerant varieties. The bushes produce nuts in little more than four years of growth and can be pruned to grow as a bush or a single-stemmed tree. Bushes grow up to 3 metres (10 feet) tall; pruning to keep them low makes harvesting easier and encourages continued growth. They will not send up new internal shoots if the base of the plant is shadowed.

Protect hazelnut bushes from deer, which love to browse on their leaves and stems, as well as from moles, voles, and mice. If hazelnuts

DAN RUBIN

are protected for the first three or four years, they generally become strong enough to survive browsing. Grimo Nut Nursery, Hardy Fruit Tree Nursery, and Whiffletree Farm and Nursery are reliable Canadian sources for seedlings. Consider these varieties of hazelnuts: Barcelona, Daviana, American, Beaked Hazel, Bush, McDonald, Epsilon, Hall's Giant, Tonda di Giffoni, and a recent hybrid, Hazelbert.

Starting with purchased rooted stock, or propagated by layering, individual hazelnuts should be planted at least 3 metres (10 feet) apart. Plants need full sun but they are quite cold-hardy. If pruned into bush form, they can create a windbreak for other plants. Hazelnuts need a steady source of moisture; plant in moist soil and provide regular irrigation to sustain the relatively shallow roots. Water them well after planting, and keep watering weekly to maintain growth and create strong roots. Once established, hazelnuts do not need much feeding, although occasional additions of nitrogen-rich materials around the plant encourages new growth.

Hazelnuts ripen in September-October and can be harvested after they fall to the ground, if animals do not eat them first. Dry them well for storage, but save some for replanting. Peel individual nuts out of their dried husks and throw the nuts into a bucket of water. Throw out those that float, since they may be empty or not viable. Keep those that sink for eating or replanting. Rodents look for nuts: protect the nuts with wire mesh.

For replanting, bury nuts in a shallow tray in damp sand and store the tray in a cool place over winter. In late winter or early spring (generally from February on), the nuts will sprout. Protect the sprouts from mice. Once they are about 13 centimetres (5 inches) tall, transplant them to containers. It takes more than a year before they are ready to plant out. Once the outdoor soil has warmed and hard frost is past, two-year-old plants can be moved outdoors, planted, and protected from browsing until they become well established.

Walnuts. Walnuts have been grown in Europe for centuries, while the closely related black walnuts are native to North America. To grow well, walnuts need protection from wind and cold and should be planted in fertile, well-drained soil. Rather than trying to grow walnuts from seed, order from a reliable nursery. Planted in a sunny, well-sheltered spot, the walnut tree will take many years to grow before producing fruit. Having harvested bags and boxes of walnuts from two trees planted by our neighbour in the Gulf

Islands of British Columbia, I can verify that these are excellent nuts to grow as a home food source. Friends in this province also have a mature walnut tree growing behind their house—but success with walnuts is a matter of finding the right tree for each location.

Butternut and Heartnut are related species to consider. Black walnuts are being grown on the west coast of the island of Newfoundland, with the promise of a harvest once the trees mature.

Almonds. Almonds are members of the same family as cherries, peaches, and plums. Like the other drupes, they produce a fleshy fruit with a seed enclosed in a woody shell. But unlike the other drupes, almonds are grown for their seed rather than fruit. Shelterwood Forest Farm in eastern Pennsylvania recommends Javid's Iranian Almond as a cold-hardy variety, and almond-peach hybrids may survive a cold winter.

29. VINES

Grapes, kiwis, and ornamental vines such as wisteria, ivy, honeysuckle, and hops can add vertical exuberance to a garden's horizontal layout, create screening for privacy, and help maximize food production. The defining quality of a vining plant is its extended stem, allowing it to grow tall and hang on or attach to a trellis or wall or other support.

Most vines prefer full sun, are vulnerable to windburn, and need support on which they can hang to continue to grow upward. Many are perennials: each year they become taller and bushier and produce many feet of vertical growth in a single year. For this reason, planting a perennial vine requires some additional consideration compared to planting a ground-hugging annual plant.

We have planted vines to create a privacy screen, for their blossoms and scent, as well as for their edible fruit. Along with vegetables, flowers, herbs, bushes, and trees, vines create a satisfying and attractive garden layout. We recommend the vines listed below.

Grapes. Research and development by Canadian and US universities has produced several northern-adapted grape varieties.

Grape vines that can endure long cold winters allow the production of grapes for eating and wine making. We recommend Lucy Kuhlman, Minnesota 78, Valiant, and other varieties. Search for grape vines that are available from growers where you live.

Kiwis. As already mentioned, northern adapted kiwis (*Actinidia arguta* and *Actinidia kolomikta*) are options for kiwi production in colder climates. Once established, after four or five years in the ground, they climb and spread out their branching vines, with the support of an appropriate wall or trellis; male and female plants are needed for pollination and fruit production. These varieties produce small, light green, lozenge-shaped fruit, which are edible as soon as they become soft. *Actinidia kolomikta* flowers' fragrance is reminiscent of that of lily of the valley. Its leaves are marked with patches of pink and silver. The fruit are elongate rather than spherical.

     DAN RUBIN

Ivy. Ivy is a perennial clinging vine that produces dark green leathery leaves and white to red or purple flowers, depending on the variety; ivy is somewhat shade-tolerant but prefers full sun to grow well. English ivy and Virginia creeper, although botanically unrelated, are both commonly called ivy. Some ivy varieties will cover the entire surface of a building, thanks to their ability to attach directly to a solid wall. The downside: most types of ivy are invasive.

Clematis. Clematis is a member of the buttercup family, a group of plants with more than 300 species; it is also known as leatherflower. Clematis produces fragrant, showy purple and white flowers and is a popular climber in temperate gardens. Clematis needs rich soil and good support to produce its full glory. It benefits from shelter from wind and prefers full sun. Planted as a screen or decorative climber, some types emit a pleasant scent when in bloom. Some types of clematis grow as shrubs rather than vines.

Wisteria. Wisteria blooms early in the year, producing white or purple-blue racemes (long strands of hanging flowers). Once mature, wisteria vines create an extravagant display of purple flowers if planted in a sheltered spot in full sun, in well-drained soil. This familiar plant is often used for decorating arches, trellises, and garden gateways and is easy to maintain with annual top-dressing and pruning.

One caution: the pods that emerge after the flowers are poisonous, so keep them away from children. A second caution: some species have become invasive. Stress such as dry soil or hot weather can induce flowering; so planting in poorer soil and providing less water can also help promote blossoms. American and Kentucky varieties are the most cold-tolerant.

Honeysuckle. Members of the genus _Lonicera_ are flowering vines with sweet-smelling flowers. Honeysuckle is the queen of flowering vines because of its persistent annual growth and the powerful scent of the flowers that appear in late summer. As a perennial, it produces masses of vines from a central stalk that becomes thicker and woodier with each passing year. We prune our honeysuckle back every year to limit this exuberant growth.

The two most common species of honeysuckle grown here are European woodbine, also known as common honeysuckle (_Lonicera periclymenum_), and American coral honeysuckle (_Lonicera sempervirens_). The first grows extremely vigorously and bears masses of fragrant, pale flowers; the second has more interesting flowers but is slow growing and scentless.

Hops. _Humulus lupulus_ is a member of the same family as cannabis and has medicinal properties. Hops were traditionally grown for their flowers, which add flavour and act as a preservative in beer. In summer, the vines extend more than 10 metres (30 feet) in height if allowed to do so and can create an annual screen. We have planted hops below our home on a rocky hillside; each year the vines grew from the ground up to the edge of the roof, more than 5 metres (16 feet), providing shade in summer and dying back each winter.

Be careful where hops are established as their cablelike underground stems spread out and are difficult to remove. But they are a reliable perennial that grows well if planted in the right place.

In 2021, for the first time, we harvested hops flowers, cutting the vines and hanging the blossoms to dry in our shed. We gave these dried flowers to a friend for use in home brewing. Their useful qualities and rapid growth make hops a valuable, multi-purpose plant.

30. WILD PLANTS IN THE GARDEN

Although you may not think of growing wild plants as part of your work in the garden, accepting the presence of well-adapted wild species is an essential part of learning to work with nature. When they appear, avoid labelling them as "weeds" and, instead, consider the benefits that these "wonderful wild plants" can offer you, as food, herbs, or a source for soil nutrients and companion plants. Every plant grows where it grows for a reason, and as we better understand this, we can tune in to the language of plants. You can rely on wild plants as indicator plants to read soil condition, nutrients, and plant needs.

Foraging for wild foods can contribute significantly to local food security, adding to our food supply wild mushrooms, herbs such as lovage, sea rocket, ox-eye daisy, mint, and chamomile, along with wonderful wild berries.

Since the 1962 publication of *Stalking the Wild Asparagus*, written by Euell Gibbons, a steady stream of books has focused on traditional knowledge. Through the centuries, Indigenous elders have collected plants and shared their knowledge.

Here in Newfoundland and Labrador, two excellent guides to wild plants are available: Peter Scott's *Edible Plants of Atlantic Canada* and Shawn Dawson's *The Forager's Dinner*, both published by Boulder Books. Even though these books can teach you about wild plants, the essential learning takes place out in the field.

Positive recognition of edible—or inedible—wild plants depends on a subtle recognition of form, location, colour, or smell. A third book to know about is *Food, Culture, Place: Stories, Traditions, and Recipes of Newfoundland* by Lori McCarthy and Marsha Tulk, a wonderfully evocative exploration of local food traditions and culture here in Newfoundland and Labrador.

When you do find wild plants growing in and around your garden, you have a chance to learn about them. They offer food and can be dried for teas or composted to create a potent fertilizer. Here are four favourite wild plants that appear in our garden each year:

Nettles. Stinging nettles leave behind an irritating reminder if you brush against the spines on their stems and leaves. Rather than cursing the "stinger nickles," it is better to regard them as indicators of good soil. Nettles, like the buttercups, dandelions, chickweed, and other wild plants we tend to remove from the garden, can be easily transformed into powerful liquid fertilizer if they are left in a bucket of water for several weeks to create a potent weed tea. The presence of nettles is a sign of nutrient-rich soil, and as they grow, they continue to build soil fertility, pulling micronutrients to the surface through their roots.

Nettles are a traditional spring tonic, easy to harvest for soups and teas. Use gloves to gather the young tips to steam or cook in soups. Nettles are even more nutritious than spinach and chard. Late in the year, when their stems become fibrous, nettles can be harvested and dried for use in herbal tea: just pull them or cut them at the base, then hang them to dry. Once they are fully dried, they lose their sting.

DAN RUBIN

Nettles were formerly grown for fabric and cordage because of their long-stapled fibres.

Chickweed. This plant sends out thin, wiry stems that support round, lobed light green leaves and tiny white flowers. Chickweed appears constantly in our salad beds, so we keep it trimmed to prevent it from overtaking our lettuce, arugula, and other salad greens. When we harvest these salad greens, we include some chickweed stems and leaves, for their interesting texture and the visual interest of small, white flowers in the salad. When the main crop is finished and the bed is ready to replant, we pull the chickweed in preparation for replanting. If kept under control, it does not need to be removed completely, since it adds to the harvest.

Nettles (top) and chickweed (bottom).

Lamb's quarters. Also known as pigweed, this wild plant in the Amaranth family has grey-green lance-shaped leathery leaves. It tastes better than spinach as a steamed green. Grown inside the protection of a cloche or a tent of plastic or floating row cover, it produces large leaves on tall stems. Closely related to quinoa, lamb's quarters has flowers that produce clustered seeds that can also be harvested and cooked.

Pineappleweed. This wild, low-growing form of chamomile pops up in the gravel along the sides of the road and in our driveway in late summer. We harvest the nubs of yellow flowers, identified by their distinctive chamomile smell, and hang them to dry indoors. Then they are mixed with dried mint and lemon balm to make Triple Tonic Tea, a winter drink that combines the gentle soothing qualities of chamomile with the zing of mint and the tangy taste of lemon balm. Pineappleweed volunteers year after year; we harvest it wherever we find it growing.

DAN RUBIN

31. THE POWER OF PUTTERING

Before we end our journey through the northern garden, there is one more way to ease your work: through the power of puttering. By spending short stretches of relaxed, unplanned time wandering through your garden, you can make note of jobs, small and large, that need to be done. If you pay attention, you will discover these details and your garden will tell you what it needs. Gardeners who are open to working with nature find new ways to adapt what they do, to better harmonize with natural processes. By spending free time in the garden, you can more easily break up the work that is needed into short, manageable tasks.

When people visit our garden and see our fruit trees and bushes, our 25 raised beds, their first comment is, "Wow, that must have been a lot of work!" Well, yes, over the past 20 years, it was a bit of work. But we did not create all these plantings in one year. Little by little, year after year, we added a bed or planted another fruit tree in the wind shadow of a mature evergreen, to create the bounty and beauty that the visitor sees.

One of the best ways to move through your garden is as an observer, noticing what the garden needs, then spontaneously weeding, pruning, thinning, or repairing as you discover what most needs attention. With the right tools, the work becomes simple and satisfying, and these small tasks do not feel like work. Of course, major projects such as building a raised bed or moving large mounds of manure can be hard physical work. But those tasks bring their own satisfaction, in tired muscles earned by moving piles of material or building new garden structures.

Through this process of puttering, I discover the work I need to do, each specific task becoming visible, as if it were rising out of the ground. I am called upon to do this work by the things I see, as I move through the landscape.

     DAN RUBIN

If we are to become partners with nature, letting wild and tame mingle and support us, we must return to our senses to see what is actually around us, putting ourselves at the service of the soil and everything that lives in it.

Moving through the garden is a journey of return, of quietly entering into a green space. It is a chance to sharpen the senses, and learn even more, while focusing on small tasks that can make a big difference to the beauty and productivity of our gardens.

32. ORGANIC, PERMACULTURE, AND REGENERATIVE GARDENING

As mentioned in the introduction, good gardeners understand that they are part of nature and succeed to the degree that they learn about and harmonize with the patterns of the living world. We need to return to that understanding.

Our big mistake as humans has been thinking that we are in charge and in control of the landscapes around us. A report released in 2022 suggests that 20 per cent of the plants, animals, fish, and birds in Canada are headed for extinction—yet another indication that we have been treating the world in the wrong way, taking too much, and ignoring the impact we are having on all living things. In case you are thinking, "Oh, more gloom and doom," let's celebrate the fact that one of the best places to restore balance and respect for life is in our own gardens.

We need to accept and understand that we are part of the living world, not separate. Even the words we use, words like "nature" and "environment," reinforce the notion that we are separate, civilized and in control. One of the things I love most about my own garden

is that it helps me see through this fallacy. My garden constantly reminds me that the world is alive and that I am just a small part of it. The more we understand and appreciate the full range of living things, the better we will be able to build fertility, food production, beauty, and healing into the landscapes we create.

By turning away from refined fertilizers and industrial poisons, by studying and recognizing the patterns of the world around us,

    DAN RUBIN

we can fit ourselves back into the structures of life and avoid a lot of unnecessary work. The goal of my workshops, and of this book, is to open eyes and inspire smiles, to understand that we have a positive role to play that will not only feed our own families but sustain all the other living things around us. So how do we do that?

Practices known as organic gardening, permaculture, and regenerative agriculture help us find the insights and techniques we need. Even though I was trained at the basic level in permaculture decades ago, I have not focused on those specific approaches in this book, leaving it to you as reader and gardener to seek out your own sources. But the techniques gained from those ways of working in the garden are woven through this book. If you are willing to learn from these garden practices and incorporate them into your work, they can help you on your way toward a healthier, more productive garden.

Organic gardening. This is the label for a way of gardening that avoids poisoning the soil with the chemicals commonly used in standard 20th- and 21st-century industrial agriculture. The Rodale Institute, a US-based family-led coalition, has been developing and sharing garden techniques that rely on adding healthy, natural ingredients to soil to build health and deter pests. In the Atlantic region of Canada, ACORN (Atlantic Canadian Organic Regional Network) embodies and supports this approach.

Organic gardening has resulted in vibrant, happy gardens around the world. A quick search will reveal books galore on the topic.

The magazine *Organic Gardening* was published by the Rodale family starting in 1942. In 1989 it was transformed into the online site *Homestead Gardening*, after achieving a monthly circulation of more than 1.5 million copies. Rodale Press has also produced a series of books, including the *Encyclopedia of Organic Gardening*. Many other authors and publishers have followed with detailed books about organic approaches to growing flowers, fruit, vegetables, greenhouse cultivation, and more. The general online source for information about garden techniques based on organic principles is rodalesoreganiclife.com, now part of the Hearst publishing empire.

Permaculture. An even deeper dive into operating in harmony with the natural world was launched by Australians Bill Mollinson and David Holmgren, who developed a system of gardening focused on sustainable, low-impact techniques to create permanent food-producing landscapes in harmony with the needs of wild plants and creatures. Permaculture is now a worldwide movement with various levels of training available.

At its core, permaculture is based on the understanding that everything is part of the living world and that we are at our best when we understand the flow of energy and water, support co-operative relationships between organisms, and respect both wild and tame while providing a place for them in our gardens. The best contact points for this approach are the Permaculture Institute and the Permaculture Institute of North America.

Regenerative agriculture. More recently, the movement toward regenerative agriculture has been transforming farms and gardens across our continent. Based on a deeper understanding of soil health and soil fertility as the source of all the food we grow on land, regenerative agriculture aims to restore the soil by the

DAN RUBIN

use of cover crops and manure and by not disturbing the soil with plowing or digging. Although these ideas are simple, efficient, and inexpensive, it is still hard for many of us to give up adding artificially created fertilizers and digging up the soil before we plant. But if we understand the soil as a living biome, we can make this transition.

Gardening can help restore fertility to the soil and health to the food we eat by harmonizing with everything that lives here. Being in the garden can become a place for endless learning; it can lead us back to ways to heal the planet while breaking through the twin illusions of separateness and control, to see our "dance in the garden" as a way of moving in harmony with everything that lives there.

INDEX

DAN RUBIN

dandelion, 61-62, 158
dill, 178
dormant oil, 56-57, 146

E
early starting, 158
earwigs, 148-49
eggplant, 197, 200, 215-17

F
fava beans, 251
feng qing choi, 163
fennel, 227
fire blight, 56, 149-50
fish waste, 41
flea beetles, 144, 148
floating row cover, 107-10
fruit, 275-301
fusarium, 150

G
garden plan, 49, 52-3
garlic, 231, 235-37
germination chart, 121
gooseberries, 279-80
goosefoot, 61 *see also* lamb's quarters
gourds, 195
grains, 265-73
grapes, 281-82, 307-8
greenhouse design, 113-19
greenhouse operation, 119, 123

H
hardening off, 135-37, 159-60
haskaps, 281
hazelnuts, 302-4
healing herbs, 183
herbs, 175-83
honeysuckle, 310
hops, 310
houseplants, 49, 131
hybrid plants, 29

I
ivy, 309

J
Jerusalem artichokes, 260-2

K
kale, 157, 164-65
kiwik, 282, 308

L
lamb's quarters, 61, 316
landscape fabric, 107
leaf miners, 148
leeks, 238-39
legumes, 243, 255
lettuce, 155-56
lovage, 228-29

M
maize, 266-67
manure, 38, 82
maple leaves, 38-9
maples, tapping, 57
marine waste, 41-42, 82-83
mealy bugs, 146
melons, 194-95
microgreens, 160-61
mildew, 149
millet, 271
mini-greenhouse, 21, 110-11
mint, 178
mizuna, 157
mould, 149
mulch/mulching, 48, 52-53, 68-69
mustard, 157
mycorrhizae, 42-43, 85

N
nasturtiums, 157
nettles, 314-15,
nightshades, 197, 217
nuts, 301-5

O
oats, 269-70
onions, 231-35
open pollination, 29
oregano, 178-79
organic gardening, 325-26
overwintering, 77

P
parsley, 178-79, 225
parsnips, 224-25
peaches, 300-301
peas, 243-49
peat, 37-38
peppers, 212-14
permaculture, 240, 326
pest control, 69, 141-51
pests, 141-51
pH, 35, 61
pigweed, 61, 272, 316
pineappleweed, 176, 316-17
plums, 298-300
pole beans, 250
potatoes, 197-98, 201-5
pruning, 55-56
pseudo-grains 265-73
pumpkins, 186-90, 192-94

Q
quince, 297-98

R
raised beds, 18, 95-101
raspberries, 280-81
red currants, 279
regenerative agriculture, 326-27
remay, 107, *see also* floating row cover
rhubarb, 282-83
root cellar, 72-74
rust fly, 144, 147
rye, 268

PHOTO CREDITS

ACKNOWLEDGEMENTS

This book is a distillation of all that I have learned in my garden since moving to the east coast of Canada in 2002. I have gained knowledge from so many other gardeners that it is hard to remember and thank them all. If you are among those who have come to my workshops and talks, then it is likely I learned something from you. We grow by sharing what we have learned.

This book could not have been assembled without the help and support of my editor Stephanie Porter and fellow gardeners and photographers Michael Burzynski, Tim Walsh, and Shawn Dawson. I have been inspired by the words and ideas of three master gardeners: Nova Scotia's Niki Jabbour; my dear friend and generous soul, Ross Traverse; and the wonderful Pat Puddester of Pat's Plants in Witless Bay, Newfoundland and Labrador.

Special thanks to Michael Burzynski for helping with text revisions, for sharing more than 100 photographs, and for providing the foreword to this book.

I have had constant support from my son, Jasper, garden helper, photographer, and co-founder of Perfectly Perennial Herbs & Seeds. My garden partner, Susan, has also provided encouragement and wisdom during the writing process.

I am one link in a family story that began with my father, Sam Rubin, who gardened and foraged in California, Europe, and Hawaii. His passion for gardening has been passed down to my daughter Ariel Rubin, who has her own beautiful Rockrose Farm, in Victoria, BC.

I owe a deep debt of gratitude to many other knowledgeable gardeners. I want to thank Wendy Bales, Stephanie Atwater, and Kate Rubin for their insight, experience, and determination to find the right way to help plants grow. I also thank friends and fellow gardeners Rena Schieck, Diane Hollett, Shawn Dawson, Philip Thornley, Megan Samms, Tom Fleming, Heather Rhodes, Elke Dettmer, Sarah Crocker, Brian Yager, Tom Loader, Nathan Gidge, Jeff Ronan, Ted Sullivan, Scott Neary, Lori McCarthy, the Walsh family, and Tom Angiers.

My final acknowledgement goes to a wonderful couple, Harry and Ethel Langmead, from whom I inherited my garden. Harry was a devoted gardener and a good friend. I am very lucky to be caring for the seaside garden that he and Ethel created, with its heritage plants, berry bushes, and fruit trees.

I am looking forward to another year of gardening beside the sea. Perhaps we will meet up along the way?

DAN RUBIN is a retired educator who makes his home in a small town north of St. John's, Newfoundland and Labrador.

Since moving to Pouch Cove in 2002, he has turned his backyard garden into a showcase for season extension, creating a small greenhouse, building raised beds, and developing shelter systems for his plants. By composting and using local materials, he has discovered easy ways to use local materials to boost soil fertility.

Through his workshops, and as operator of a heritage seed company, Perfectly Perennial Herbs and Seeds, Dan has been inspiring a return to self-sufficiency and homegrown food.

He is the author of six books, dozens of articles and short stories, and award-winning poetry. A composer, his original music has been released on 14 acoustic albums that he has recorded with friends.

In 2022, Dan was recognized as a Community Champion by the Dean of the Faculty of Medicine at Memorial University for his work as founder and chairperson of Food Producers Forum, a provincial non-profit helping restore local food production and food justice.

*You feed the garden,
then the garden
feeds you.*